STEVE BACKLUND

WITH JARED NEUSCH
featuring Jesse Cupp, Wendee Fiscus and Anna Flory

Higher
PERSPECTIVES

© copyright 2012 Steve Backlund, Igniting Hope Ministries
www.IgnitedHope.com

Cover Design : Linda Lee www.LindaLeeCreates.com
Interior Design and Formatting : Lorraine Box PropheticArt@sbcglobal.net

Many thanks to the following people for their input in the writing of these devotionals: Holly Hayes, Kim Jaramillo, and Julie Mustard.

ISBN: 978-0-9854773-5-6

dedicated to...

Paul Manwaring

Thanks for your heart to father many, your influence
in authentic leadership, and for your belief in me.
It is a joy to work with you.

Senior Pastors Around the World

You are my heroes for answering the prayer of Jesus
for laborers (shepherds) for the harvest.
I am committed to helping you
and your ministries be strong.

endorsements

I have known Steve Backlund for several decades. His outlook on life is truly contagious. A man possessed by hope and faith, he serves the people of God once again with another great book, *Higher Perspectives*, that demonstrates how a man of his stature looks at life. A renewed mind is one of the most vital aspects of the Christian walk. Our awareness of how God thinks and views life determines our effectiveness in this world. Dissecting examples throughout Scripture, Steve Backlund and his team challenge readers to recognize the lies that they may be believing and exchange them for the Higher Perspective of how God sees. This book is a great tool in the quest for all believers to continually renew their mind and see as the Father sees.

Bill Johnson
Senior Leader, Bethel Church, Redding, California

The average person today hears more bad news in one week than someone just 50 years ago would have heard in his or her entire lifetime. Without even realizing it, most Christians have been boiled in the oil of skepticism, pessimism and negativism. This has resulted in faithless Christianity... unbelieving believers struggling through life carrying a deep sense of hopelessness and foreboding. Yet in the midst of this tumultuous age, God has seated us in heavenly places, empowering us to have timeless perspectives as well as supernatural solutions.

Steve Backlund's book *Higher Perspectives* is a training manual for God's reigning royalty. It's a 50-day devotional dedicated to transforming our minds so that we can view life through God's eternal perspectives, and bring hope to this desperate and dying planet. Every Christian needs to read this devotional! Without question, this book will change your thinking and transform the world around you.

Kris Vallotton
Senior Associate Leader, Bethel Church, Redding, California
Co-Founder of *Bethel School of Supernatural Ministry*
Author of eight books including *The Supernatural Ways of Royalty* and *Spirit Wars*

God bless you as you enter the Elevator of *Higher Perspectives*. Prepare yourself for a challenge in how you experience life from now on. Few people know how to put circumstances under their feet like Steve Backlund and his teams. I am excited for anyone who reads this book or any others by this author. I love how much hope fills the lives of the readers and listeners of Steve's ministry.

Danny Silk
Sr. Leadership Team, Bethel Church, Redding, California
Author of *Culture of Honor* and *Loving Our Kids On Purpose*

The combination of this book's title, knowing the man who wrote it, and the layout and content of the book itself create the best endorsement. *Higher Perspectives* is sincerely inviting as a title, and Steve, who I know well, lives the title well. Not only that, but the book is laid out to be practical, feeding the reader in bite-size chunks. All of these combine in a recipe that will enhance your life. You may never meet Steve in person, but you will meet him through this book. This is him: a man, of the Word of God, practical applications, and a life of pursuit and leading others in heir own pursuit, and, in this case, leading others to a Higher Perspective.

Paul Manwaring
Global Legacy, Bethel Church, Redding, California

Often times a reader will get a book and read it and walk away with the struggle to find a way to apply it to their own personal life. This is one of the reasons I really appreciate Steve Backlund and his approach to teaching and writing. In his new book *Higher Perspectives*, he takes you on a journey to help you literally think and live higher in your daily life. I was moved by the examples and the practical nature of the book. There is no question I will encourage people to read *Higher Perspectives*.

Eric Johnson
Local Church Senior Leader, Bethel Church, Redding, California

The book *Higher Perspectives*, is more than just a book — It is a journey into new levels of living an overcoming victorious life. Steve Backlund, along with his interns, have revealed key core value Kingdom truths that will lead you into new levels of freedom and breakthrough. The higher perspectives outlined in each chapter are not just theoretical thoughts or fanciful philosophies, but Biblical insights into the Father's heart, revealing a vision of how He views things from His perspective. The higher perspective is God's perspective from Heaven looking down upon earth. If we want to be those who experience "Your Kingdom come, Your will be done on earth as it is in Heaven" (Matthew 6:9), then we must have a proper perspective of the vantage point from Heaven. This book will help you to become a Kingdom minded person, so that you can release God's Kingdom in and through your life. This book is a must read for those who want to know the truth that sets us free!

Kevin Dedmon

Firestarters, Bethel Church, Redding, California

Author, *The Ultimate Treasure Hunt: Supernatural Evangelism Through Supernatural Encounters*

Higher Perspectives is not just an incredible devotional, or great curriculum for a small group, but reading it with Holy Spirit will bring a strategic shift to your perspectives and reality. Steve Backlund and his team have done it again, he's written a profoundly powerful, life-changing book in a simple and understandable format.

Barry & Lori Byrne

Founders, *Love After Marriage International*

Steve and his team have done it again — given us a profoundly practical tool for accessing the abundant life! Each short devotional exposes the robbers of right living and displaces them with divinely-inspired declarations and easy-to-follow action steps. *Higher Perspectives* cuts the tether of limitations tied to earthbound ideas and releases the reader to the potent potential of the truly renewed mind.

Colossians tells us that "all the treasures of wisdom and knowledge are hidden in the person of Christ Jesus." Those who dare to "set their minds on things above" will find themselves accessing the available genius of the mind of Christ. *Higher Perspectives* is a tuning fork releasing the resonant frequencies of heavenly realities.

I've had the honor of observing Steve Backlund's journey from glory to glory for more than a decade. I know him as a man of integrity who builds leaders and transforms communities. Steve has a unique ability to manage personal disciplines with boundless delight. This being true, I believe the concepts of this book are not some empty ideals on a page but a tried and true road map offering transformational landmarks from Steve's own personal Kingdom quest. I strongly recommend that every believer take the high road of *Higher Perspectives*.

Dan (Dano) McCollam

Director of *Sounds of the Nations*, and core team of The Mission, Vacaville, California

Global Legacy Apostolic Team, Faculty teacher at *Bethel School of the Prophets*,

Bethel School of Worship, and *Deeper School of the Supernatural*

Author, *Basic Training for Prophetic Activation*

contents

PERSPECTIVE

Additional Resources by Steve & Wendy Backlund

about the authors

Steve Backlund

Steve Backlund was a senior pastor for seventeen years before joining the team at Bethel Church (Redding, California) in 2008. Ten of those years were spent on the backside of the desert in Central Nevada where he and his wife, Wendy Backlund, led their church into renewal and significant growth.

In 2001 Bill Johnson and Kris Vallotton called Steve and Wendy to be senior leaders at Mountain Chapel in Weaverville, California (the church that Bill pastored for seventeen years). As a result of these experiences, Steve and Wendy developed a special heart for senior leaders and other church leaders which led them to their current position at Bethel Church which focuses on leader development in Bethel School of Supernatural Ministry and through online curriculum for leaders around the world.

Jared Neusch, *2011 intern*

Jared oversees the third year interns at *Bethel School of Supernatural Ministry*. In addition to working in the school, he travels in ministry with his wife Kezia, and assists Steve in writing projects. He is originally from Texas and his heart has always been for the church to succeed. He most comes alive when he teaches, travels, and writes.

Jesse Cupp, *2012 intern*

Jesse assists Steve in Global Legacy as a Regional Catalyst, with the goal of strengthening the apostolic relational network and catalyzing the revival movement. He grew up in Indiana, and has served the Lord living in Tennessee, Hawaii, and California. He married his beautiful wife, Jessica, in 2005, and they look forward to many more years of bringing revival to the Body of Christ and harvesting the nations.

Wendee Fiscus, *2012 intern*

Wendee assists Steve with his marketing and the Leadership Development Program in Global Legacy. She also works for a magazine publishing company, where she enjoys connecting with clients regarding marketing and sales. Wendee is originally from San Diego and has a heart to see the body of Christ come to their full potential and identity in Him.

Anna Maher, *2012 intern*

Anna serves Global Legacy through helping establish greater connection among churches on a regional level; additionally, she oversees members of Steve's intern team. Anna is originally from Texas, and worked with Youth With A Mission prior to coming to Bethel. She has a heart for the nations and preparing a radiant Bride for His return. Anna and her husband, Chuck, travel equipping the church to live the abundant life.

foundational truths
for this book

1. **Our conclusions about circumstances are more important than the circumstances themselves.**
   The experience of the twelve spies in Numbers 13 is a classic illustration of this. Two groups of people saw the exact same set of circumstances and put a different conclusion on what they saw. Their "perspective" affected their personal destinies, as well as that of the nation of Israel. Joshua and Caleb saw the circumstances through God's promises, while the other ten saw through the lens of an untrustworthy God and their own perceived inadequacies. We have the spiritual DNA of Joshua and Caleb, not the ten spies. This book will help release the grace for us to see and experience life as Joshua and Caleb did.

2. **God's perspective on circumstances is higher than ours, and it is always filled with hope.**
   "For as the heavens are higher than the earth, so are my ways higher than your ways, and my thoughts than your thoughts" (Isaiah 55:9). "Now may the God of hope fill you with all joy and peace in believing, that you may abound in hope by the power of the Holy Spirit" (Romans 15:13). We have been given "exceedingly great and precious promises, that through these you may be partakers of the divine nature" (2 Peter 1:4).

3. **The higher perspectives recorded in Scripture are invitations for us to live at greater levels.**
   "I have come that they may have life, and that they may have

it more abundantly" (John 10:10). The scriptural examples this book highlights invite us to believe what was believed and to experience what was experienced. They are not simply to be read as interesting history, but to be lived.

4. **We are on a journey to become fully convinced of God's perspective.**

Abraham is our role model teaching us to understand that possessing higher perspectives is an ongoing process, not a one-time event. "(Abraham) ...was strengthened in faith, giving glory to God, and being fully convinced that what He had promised He was also able to perform" (Romans 4:20-21). Abraham did not dwell on the problem, but focused on God (giving glory to God). This book will help you do the same and strengthen your faith so that you will become fully persuaded to see yourself, others and circumstances through God's eyes.

5. **Current beliefs create future experience.**

"And do not be conformed to this world, but be transformed by the renewing of your mind" (Romans 12:2). Whatever perspective we renew our minds with today will transform our experience tomorrow. When I (Steve) first understood this, it discouraged me (because my circumstances then showed that I must have some really bad beliefs!). But then I got encouraged, because I realized that I could "think on purpose" and transform my tomorrows. So can you! You are an Abraham to your generation.

understanding
the six components of each page

The Higher Perspective

This is a direct quote from either a biblical author or someone he records in scripture.

Verse & Context

The situation and verses that surround the higher perspective is explained.

Lower Perspectives

We list what would be common ways of thinking regarding the subject being addressed. We introduce these sometimes humorous viewpoints with the phrase "this person should have concluded..." We are not denying the "facts" of situations, but we use these lower perspectives to jolt us out of low level thinking to believe God's promises.

Elevating Truths

Higher perspectives result from believing truth in a greater way. The elevating truths are keys to becoming fully convinced and thus being able to live the abundant life that Jesus promised He came to give (John 10:10).

Giving God Something To Work With

In John 2, Jesus, the One with the highest perspectives on the planet, did not create wine out of thin air. He brought transformation in a circumstance by asking for something to work with. He basically said, "Give Me those pots, and give me some water. I need something to work with for a miracle to happen." In giving God something the work with, we also need to add substantive action to our higher perspectives to see real breakthrough. Indeed, "faith without works is dead." (See James 2:17)

Declarations To Create Higher Perspectives

God's way of bringing life to dead places, "dead" people, and dead areas of your life is to call them alive before they are manifesting life. It is what the angel of the Lord did to a "dead" leader named Gideon. He called him a great leader before he was a great leader. This truth is reinforced by a phrase in Joel 3:10 – "Let the weak say, 'I am strong.'" The weak cannot simply wait for someone else to tell him he is strong, but he is to speak the word of strength over himself while still experiencing weakness. He does not deny his experience but he also does not create his identity from it. He is to agree with God's word, not his past. He is to prophesy over himself because "faith comes by hearing" (Romans 10:17). What we hear over and over, we will start believing. It is one of God's main ways for us to demolish negative strongholds and establish new, positive ones. This is why declarations are such an important part of Higher Perspectives.

50

Higher

PERSPECTIVES

all things are possible to him who believes

*"So (Jesus) asked his father, 'How long has this been happening to (your son)?' And he said, 'From childhood. And often he has thrown him both into the fire and into the water to destroy him. But if You can do anything, have compassion on us and help us.' Jesus said to him, 'If you can believe, **all things are possible to him who believes.'** Immediately the father of the child cried out and said with tears, 'Lord, I believe; help my unbelief!'"*

Mark 9:21-24

Lower Perspectives

The boy's father could have concluded:

- There were no solutions because of how long this problem existed.

- Jesus got a little carried away in the moment and really meant to say that a few small things are possible if God is in a good mood that day.

- Begging Jesus is more vital than believing in the person of Jesus.

- God is not that concerned about children being emotionally free.

- Jesus was insensitive to focus on his level of faith.

- Declaring "Lord, I believe!" was a lie. His experience proved otherwise.

Elevating Truths

1. **A main key to overcoming obstacles is to develop our beliefs** – The father said to Jesus, "But if You can do anything, have compassion on us and help us." Jesus turned the focus from divine willingness and ability to the father's personal beliefs. Jesus said, "If you can believe, all things are possible to him who believes." The father was invited into a higher perspective that

would change everything.

2. **The duration of a problem does not determine the likelihood of breakthrough** – The Bible frequently reported the time span of an unresolved difficulty to stir hope in us that long-standing issues have solutions (and are still to be pursued for a miracle). A negative perspective about apparent unmovable situations is a bigger problem than the problem.

3. **Jesus is the author and finisher of our faith** – "Immediately the father of the child cried out and said with tears, 'Lord, I believe; help my unbelief!'" This man of seemingly small faith received a great miracle because of his humility and for "looking unto Jesus, the author and finisher of (his) faith" (Hebrews 12:2). We can do the same.

Giving God Something to Work With

- **Memorize** Romans 12:2 and John 8:31-32.

- **Cry out to God for a revolution** to happen in your beliefs about a long-standing issue.

- **Take a specific step** toward bringing freedom to children and youth.

Declarations to Create Higher Perspectives

Jesus is the author and finisher of my faith.

God has surprising solutions to my long-standing concerns.

My faith brings freedom to my children.

2   if only
I may touch His garment

A woman overcomes past disappointment and current obstacles to access God's power in an incredible way. *"And suddenly, a woman who had a flow of blood for twelve years came from behind and touched the hem of His garment. For she said to herself, 'If only I may touch His garment, I shall be made well.' But Jesus turned around, and when He saw her He said, 'Be of good cheer, daughter; your faith has made you well.' And the woman was made well from that hour."*

Matthew 9:20-22

Lower Perspectives
This woman could have concluded:

- If Jesus wanted to heal her, He would come to her.
- She was predestined by God to have the quality of life she had.
- There was nothing she could do to change her circumstances.
- Healing was unlikely because it was a long-standing issue.
- If God wanted her to experience breakthrough, there would not be obstacles in her way.
- It would be unwise for her to get her hopes up again.
- She should ask Jesus if He wanted to heal her.

Elevating Truths

1. **There is always a solution for every situation** – "No temptation has overtaken you except such as is common to man; but God is faithful, who will not allow you to be tempted beyond what you are able, but with the temptation will also make the way of escape, that you may be able to bear it" (I Corinthians 10:13). There is a way to experience breakthrough. Believing this will draw the solution to you.

2. **Spiritual hunger and spiritual tenacity bring great rewards** – "He is a rewarder of those who diligently seek Him" (Hebrews 11:6). "Draw near to God and He will draw near to you" (James 4:8). "And let us not grow weary while doing good, for in due season we shall reap if we do not lose heart" (Galatians 6:9).

3. **We are not predestined to hardship or mediocrity** – Our Lord has no partiality. God is a "whosoever" God. "For 'whoever calls on the name of the LORD shall be saved'" (Romans 10:13). The word "saved" comes from the Greek word sozo that means saved, healed and delivered.

Giving God Something to Work With

- **Go to locations** where God is moving in powerful ways.
- **Speak words of hope and faith.** She said, "If I only touch His garment I will be made well."
- **Pursue breakthrough** in a long-lasting situation.

Declarations to Create Higher Perspectives

There is always a solution.

I live a life of great spiritual hunger and tenacity.

I will increasingly experience every aspect of the salvation that Jesus won for me.

bringing every thought into captivity to Christ

*"For the weapons of our warfare are not carnal but mighty in God for pulling down strongholds, casting down arguments and every high thing that exalts itself against the knowledge of God, **bringing every thought into captivity to the obedience of Christ.**"*

2 Corinthians 10:4-5

Lower Perspectives

We could conclude:

- We are powerless to change negative thinking patterns.

- Past behavior is a bigger problem than current beliefs.

- Pulling down strongholds is only about defeating regional demonic activity.

- Christians should be more concerned about what they believe during prayer than after prayer.

- The renewing of the mind in Romans 12:2 is a good spiritual discipline but does not bring transformation.

- The devil is a bigger problem to us than our current beliefs.

Elevating Truths

1. **Know we can change what we think and believe** – "Finally, brethren, whatever things are true, whatever things are noble... whatever things are of good report... meditate (think) on these things" (Philippians 4:8). God always provides power to do what He commands.

2. **Believing truth obliterates lies and creates hope-filled thoughts** – "Now may the God of hope fill you with all joy and peace in believing" (Romans 15:13). The two key words of this verse are "in believing." The moment we believe truth, we are infused with the capacity for abundant hope. Assuredly, "the

truth shall make you free" (John 8:32). We start our journey to freedom by capturing hopeless thoughts with truth.

3. **Renewing our minds today will cause transformation tomorrow** – "Be transformed by the renewing of your mind" (Romans 12:2) is one of the most potential-packed phrases in the Bible. By renewing our minds today our lives and circumstances will be revolutionized in the future.

Giving God Something to Work With

- **Listen to messages regularly** that build hope and faith.
- **Read out loud a list of declarations** every morning and evening.
- **Memorize and meditate** much on Scripture.

Declarations to Create Higher Perspectives

I am pulling down strongholds of wrong beliefs fueled by lies.

My thoughts are increasingly hope-filled.

My powerful beliefs and prayers are dislodging demonic activity in my region.

*"Then David said to the Philistine, 'You come to me with a sword, with a spear, and with a javelin. But I come to you in the name of the LORD of hosts, the God of the armies of Israel, whom you have defied. **This day the LORD will deliver you into my hand,** and I will strike you and take your head from you. And this day I will give the carcasses of the camp of the Philistines to the birds of the air and the wild beasts of the earth, that all the earth may know that there is a God in Israel.'"*

1 Samuel 17:45-46

Lower Perspectives

David could have concluded:

- God should have chosen someone older or bigger who could fill his armor to have a better shot against Goliath.

- Because he had never fought in a real battle, he should be terrified.

- Because Goliath was so big, he and the Israelites should believe he was sent from God to humble them as punishment.

- Doing small things in a great way his whole life was all for nothing.

- It was prideful and foolish for him to step out in courage without multiple signs from God or hearing His audible voice.

Elevating Truths

1. **Our struggle is not against flesh and blood** – David was well aware that muscle, size and weaponry had little to do with this battle. If in life we look to the physical realm to draw our hope, many times we will live depressed. Ephesians 6:12 tells us that our struggle is not against flesh and blood, but that we are fighting a spiritual battle. Goliath may have been a physical giant, but God was behind David, a spiritual giant.

2. **God is on our side** – David's confident claim was rooted in the power of God to deliver, not in his ability to fight. Romans 8:31 says, "If God is for us, who can be against us?" This is great news: God is for you! With that revelation, what "Goliaths" are you going to run at today?

3. **Testimonies build courage** – A big part of David's courage was remembering his past victories against the lion and the bear. Keeping a journal of past victories, big or small, is vital when we face "Goliaths."

Giving God Something to Work With

- **Focus on doing one thing very well** (as David did with his slingshot).
- **Speak God's promises** to the Goliaths in your life.
- **Study the lives of giant killers.**

Declarations to Create Higher Perspectives

I am a giant killer.

I run at my "Goliaths."

I release breakthrough for entire nations.

5 he knelt down on his knees three times a day and prayed

"So these governors and satraps said (to the king): 'King Darius, live forever... make a firm decree, that whoever petitions any god or man for thirty days, except you, O king, shall be cast into the den of lions.' King Darius signed the written decree. Now when Daniel knew that the writing was signed, ... **he knelt down on his knees three times that day, and prayed** *and gave thanks before his God, as was his custom since early days."*

Daniel 6:6-10

Lower Perspectives

Daniel could have concluded:

- He should quit praying because all the difficulty he was experiencing showed that prayer was not making any difference.

- God was punishing some previous sin in his life.

- He should be scared because nowhere in the Bible had anyone ever been saved from a lion's den.

- God was being unfair to him and had turned His back on him.

- If they asked him not to pray, they must have a good reason for it.

- He should worry because even God doesn't know how to overturn a signed decree by the king.

Elevating Truths

1. **Thankfulness is a lifestyle, not an emotion** – Knowing that his life was on the line, Daniel went straight home, and with his windows open, prayed and gave thanks before God. Seasons in life may shift, but thankfulness is a constant. Even in arguably one of his scariest times, Daniel knew to spend time thanking God.

2. **God radically rewards faithfulness** – Sometimes being faithful

PERSPECTIVES

is underestimated or can feel overlooked if there isn't an instant recognition or fruit. In the Kingdom, however, faithfulness builds compound interest. God defended Moses, explaining that He spoke to him face to face because of his faithfulness (Numbers 12:7, 8). Even when threatened, Daniel was faithful to pray as he had done since his youth.

3. **Prayer is a powerful force** – When Jesus taught His disciples how to pray in Matthew 6, He was positioning them for power, intimacy, access to heaven, and so much more. Faced with a choice, Daniel wagered that maintaining a consistent prayer life was worth losing his own life. Daniel was someone who lived with a mighty conviction of the power of prayer, and that the fruit is overwhelming (Daniel 6:18-28).

Giving God Something to Work With

-   **Increase thankfulness to God and people.** It is a gateway into greater things. (See Psalms 100:4.)
-   **Stay committed to all types of prayer** in every way possible.
-   **Stand up for something** you believe in.

Declarations to Create Higher Perspectives

I have non-negotiable convictions.

I am a person of great prayer and gratitude.

God gets behind my quality decisions by bringing great breakthrough.

give Your servant an understanding heart to judge Your people

*"At Gibeon the Lord appeared to Solomon in a dream… and said, 'Ask! What shall I give you?' And Solomon said: 'You have shown great mercy to Your servant David my father… and You have given him a son to sit on his throne, as it is this day. Now, O Lord my God… I am a little child; I do not know how to go out or come in… Therefore **give to Your servant an understanding heart to judge Your people** that I may discern between good and evil. For who is able to judge this great people of Yours?'"*

I Kings 3:5-9

Lower Perspectives

Solomon could have concluded:

- He should not get his hopes up because this was only a dream.

- God will be angry if his answer is not that he wants "more love" for God.

- He should ask for all the power and wealth on the planet because those things would bring satisfaction and happiness.

- He couldn't ask for much because he was not worthy of anything big.

- God must have had "strings attached" that he was not aware of.

Elevating Truths

1. **God is a good God** – In Matthew 7:11, Jesus says, "If you then, being evil, know how to give good gifts to your children, how much more will your Father who is in heaven give good things to those who ask Him!" God is a good God who loves to give good gifts to His children. Believing this truth changes what you expect, which will change what you receive.

2. **You are worthy to be blessed** – When Jesus became our sacrifice on the cross, He instantly received what we deserved so

Higher
PERSPECTIVES

that we could get what He deserves. As believers, we can expect blessings around every corner, not because of what we earn, but because of what He earned through a sinless life. We have been drafted into His lineage and blessing is our inheritance.

3. **Wisdom should be desired** – Proverbs 2 goes into great depth about the extreme blessing that comes from wisdom. (See James 1:5-8 also.) Valuing wisdom positions us to be blessed in many other areas.

Giving God Something to Work With

- **Ask God for bigger things** than you think you deserve.
- **Meditate on James 1:5.** Then ask God for profound wisdom. Thank Him every day that more is coming.
- **Write down a new idea daily.**

Declarations to Create Higher Perspectives

I walk in supernatural wisdom.

God loves to give good things to me.

I am 100% worthy in Jesus for all of God's best blessings.

My wisdom and many resources bless others greatly.

7 I will not let You go unless You bless me

*"Then Jacob was left alone; and a Man wrestled with him until the breaking of day... And (the angel) said, 'Let me go...' But (Jacob) said, **'I will not let You go unless You bless me.'** So He said to him...'Your name shall no longer be called Jacob, but Israel.'"*

Genesis 32:24-28

Lower Perspectives

Jacob could have concluded:

- He had already been blessed by Isaac, so there was no need to try and get more blessing.

- Because he was deceitful in getting his last blessing, God would be too angry to release another blessing over him.

- He should let this Man go or He will probably curse him.

- Giving him a new name wasn't a blessing; it was just God's way of weaseling out of the situation.

- He should see the angel's desire to go as a heavenly command, not a heavenly test.

Elevating Truths

1. **Blessing is powerful** – Jacob went to extreme measures to attain blessing. He was well aware that "blessing" was more than just a courtesy gesture after a sneeze. It's time we were more excited about a blessing than scared of a curse. Raising your expectation about the power of blessing positions you to receive the benefits.

2. **Persistence is rewarded** – In Luke 18, Jesus tells the story of the persistent widow. The widow was avenged because of her continued persistence. While it is key to live from a place of rest, it's important to realize that rest isn't the absence of activity; It's

the presence of peace. Even though sometimes we have legal ownership of something, we are still called to actively go get it!

3. **Your past does not define your future** – Jacob could have given up from birth by simply realizing that his name meant he would always come in second place. Rather, Jacob acted powerfully, understanding that his past didn't steer his future - his beliefs did. Keeping his past where it belonged (behind him), Jacob pursued blessing and got a name-change. Your beliefs, not your past, determine your destiny.

Giving God Something to Work With

- **Make a habit** of consistently releasing blessing on those around you.
- **Raise your expectations** when someone blesses you.
- **Ask God how to actively pursue a desire in your heart.**

Declarations to Create Higher Perspectives

I am a magnet for blessing.

I am a powerful and active Christian.

*My life is dramatically changing for the better
because I have been blessed by God through Jesus Christ.*

8
for God sent me before you to preserve life

*"So... Joseph made himself known to his brothers. And Joseph said to his brothers, 'Please come near to me.' So they came near. Then he said: 'I am Joseph your brother, whom you sold into Egypt. But now, do not therefore be grieved or angry with yourselves because you sold me here; **for God sent me before you to preserve life...** So now it was not you who sent me here, but God.'"*

Genesis 45:1-8

Lower Perspectives

Joseph could have concluded:

- Because it would be convenient, this opportunity to get revenge on his brothers must be from God and therefore the best option.

- He was not lovable because his brothers hated him.

- He should never trust his brothers again because if he restores intimacy with them, they'll probably end up betraying him.

- His brothers must have been sent back into his life because he needed to go back through another painful process of betrayal.

- God cannot turn the mistreatment he experienced into the launching pad for his life's purpose.

Elevating Truths

1. **Forgiveness is key in the Kingdom** – Forgiveness is not just something Jesus does. We have been commissioned into the same ministry (Matthew 6:15). Part of daily life is extending radical forgiveness to others, not because we think they deserve it, but because He forgave us first.

2. **Embracing the process brings promotion** – Usually the process is more important than our perceived destination. If Joseph, the young, passionate dreamer, had skipped his process, promotion

would more than likely have crushed him. He was able to be inwardly successful, even though it appeared outwardly like he was not successful. Welcoming and understanding process equips you to succeed in whatever, wherever, and however God wants to use you. Although God does not cause bad things to happen, He can use them.

3. **God is doing more than we think** – Joseph had no idea what God had planned for his family. Regardless of what your current circumstances or your past experiences may be telling you, God is always doing more than meets the eye. Understanding this powerful truth releases hope and helps us war against hopelessness and depression.

Giving God Something to Work With

- **Start speaking blessings** over difficult people in your life.
- **Increase your thankfulness** during hard seasons.
- **Apply faith** to a seemingly impossible situation.

Declarations to Create Higher Perspectives

I am quick to forgive people when they have wronged me.

I have a great perspective of the bigger picture God is doing in my life.

I welcome and embrace process.

9 my lord, may the dream concern those who hate you

Babylonian King Nebuchadnezzar had a dream that upset him. None of his astrologers and magicians could interpret it. He asked Daniel, a Jewish captive whom he respected, for its interpretation. Daniel understood it and became undone by its negative implications for Nebuchadnezzar. *"Then Daniel, whose name was Belteshazzar, was astonished for a time, and his thoughts troubled him. So the king spoke, and said, 'Belteshazzar, do not let the dream or its interpretation trouble you.' Belteshazzar answered and said, **'My lord, may the dream concern those who hate you,** and its interpretation concern your enemies!'"*

Daniel 4:19

Lower Perspectives

Daniel could have concluded:

- Nebuchadnezzar was only getting what he deserved, and it would be a good thing for him to be judged.

- God loves the poor and needy, but does not like the rich and powerful.

- It was impossible for this heathen king to have a life-changing and nation-changing encounter with God.

- God hated Babylon and this king for what they did to the Jewish people.

- Because Nebuchadnezzar had beliefs and political views contrary to Scripture, Daniel should picket the king's palace.

Elevating Truths

1. **We can bloom wherever we are planted** – Daniel could have been embittered that he was born in a difficult time. Instead, he heeded Jeremiah's call to thrive in current situations and be a mighty influence for God. (See Jeremiah 29:1-14.) We can do the same.

PERSPECTIVES

2. **Compassion for people creates the environment for miracles –** Effective ministry to people results from a compassionate love for people. Our focus is not how God feels about our ministry. Our focus is how God feels about those we are seeking to help.

3. **The influential are still having dreams and encounters with God still today –** As we walk in integrity, love and a strong identity, we will be the ones that reveal Christ and Kingdom purposes to them.

Giving God Something to Work With

- **Learn to honor and support leaders** you disagree with.
- **Be a part of a prayer meeting** for leaders. (1 Timothy 2:1-4)
- **Find ways to leave every environment better** than you found them.

Declarations to Create Higher Perspectives

I have a heart of compassion for all, including the influential.

I have favor with political leaders.

I interpret dreams of influential people.

the fellowship
of His sufferings

*"Yet indeed I also count all things loss for the excellence of the knowledge of Christ Jesus my Lord, for whom I have suffered the loss of all things, and count them as rubbish, that I may gain Christ and be found in Him, not having my own righteousness, which is from the law, but that which is through faith in Christ, the righteousness which is from God by faith; that I may know Him and the power of His resurrection, and the **fellowship of His sufferings**, being conformed to His death."*

Philippians 3:8-10

Lower Perspectives

Paul could have concluded:

- Suffering only results from believing lies and is never beneficial to spiritual growth.

- We should enjoy the benefits that others have helped create but be unconcerned about increasing those benefits for future generations.

- Christians should only do what is popular.

- There is nothing to overcome on the journey to becoming a leader.

Elevating Truths

1. **Great love lays its life down for others** – "This is My commandment, that you love one another as I have loved you. Greater love has no one than this, than to lay down one's life for his friends" (John 15:12-13). Just as a nation's freedom results from sacrifice, spiritual freedom advances when those on the front lines are willing to pay a price in prayer, integrity, truth, shepherding people, and even martyrdom.

2. **Prophetic vision for our lives fuels rigorous spiritual training –** Athletes "punish" their bodies because they dream of victory and success. We too exercise ourselves unto godliness by pressing against personal and spiritual resistance to have the "muscles" to help bring corporate victory tomorrow. Indeed, our current battles are not just about us but about those who will experience breakthrough because of our victories.

3. **Spiritual reformers are often reviled –** The Jews persecuted Paul. Many hated Martin Luther, the Protestant reformer. We cannot be dismayed by negative reactions as we teach and demonstrate neglected biblical truths.

Giving God Something to Work With

- **Determine daily to contribute** more than you take wherever you are.
- **Gorge on messages** that will inspire radical personal growth.
- **Focus more on people respecting you than liking you.**

Declarations to Create Higher Perspectives

I have beliefs I would die for.

I am an overcomer.

My victories create breakthrough for many others.

11 a thousand may fall at your side...
but it shall not come near you

*"He who dwells in the secret place of the Most High shall abide under the shadow of the Almighty. I will say of the LORD, 'He is my refuge and my fortress; my God, in Him I will trust.' Surely He shall deliver you from the snare of the fowler and from the perilous pestilence... You shall not be afraid of the terror by night, nor of the arrow that flies by day, nor of the pestilence that walks in darkness, nor of the destruction that lays waste at noonday. **A thousand may fall at your side, and ten thousand at your right hand; but it shall not come near you.**"*

Psalm 91:1-7

Lower Perspectives

The Psalmist could have concluded:

- He could not possibly know what would happen in the future.
- God's plan for them may be to die in battle so he should not say this.
- There are no extraordinary benefits to being God's son or daughter.
- He should not make such a powerful statement because he might be considered proud or an embracer of positive confession teaching.
- Current beliefs and declarations don't affect future experience.

Elevating Truths

1. **Increased protection results from kingdom advancement –** The overall teaching of Scripture is that God's people will have protection in their lives and families. It is part of being blessed (see Deuteronomy 28), and it is part of kingdom advancement (see 1 Timothy 2:1-2).

2. **Unusual and miraculous protection is available to all believers –** Daniel, David, the three Hebrew children, Jesus and Paul experienced supernatural protection. Their lives are an invitation for us to discover what they believed and experienced.

3. **Declaring supernatural protection over others helps them to experience it** – Proclaiming the highest possibilities in Christ is needed for us to live at the uppermost level of living. (See Galatians 3:5, Romans 10:17.) Something powerful happens when we proclaim to others the exceeding and abundant things of God. (See Ephesians 3:20).

Giving God Something to Work With

- **Memorize Psalm 91:1-16.**

- **Talk more about protection** than spiritual attacks. As you do, you will sow seeds into your own future protection.

- **Flood scriptural promises** into your prayers, prophecies, declarations, conversations and teachings.

Declarations to Create Higher Perspectives

I live under supernatural protection.

My life has stories of remarkable protection.

My encouragement of others
with the promise of God changes their lives.

12 Mary took very costly oil and wiped His feet with her hair

"Jesus came to Bethany, where Lazarus was who had been dead ...There they made Him a supper; and Martha served, but Lazarus was one of those who sat at the table with Him. **Then Mary took a pound of very costly oil of spikenard, anointed the feet of Jesus, and wiped His feet with her hair** *...But one of his disciples, Judas Iscariot ...said, 'Why was this fragrant oil not sold for 300 denarii and given to the poor?' ...But Jesus said, 'Let her alone ...For the poor you have with you always, but Me you do not have always.'"*

John 12:1-8

Lower Perspectives

Mary could have concluded:

- All extra money and resources should always be given to the poor.
- Judas was the treasurer; therefore, his perspective must be right.
- The only thing Jesus hates more than rejecting the poor is being wasteful. She is in deep trouble.
- Jesus does not respond to extravagant acts of love.
- Jesus prefers that we serve Him, not lavish our love on Him.

Elevating Truths

1. **We are lovers of Christ** – We are betrothed to Christ, and are lovers. In Scripture, we're called children, friends, kings and queens, but most importantly, lovers. It's in our very nature to extravagantly love Him. "We love Him because He first (extravagantly) loved us" (1 John 4:19).

2. **Giving should be from Spirit overflow** – Giving was never meant to be legalistic or compulsory. (See 2 Corinthians 9:7.) In that moment, Judas was operating from law, and Mary was

tapped into what the Spirit was doing. When we give, we are not primarily motivated by need but by overflowing love through the Spirit.

3. **God is a God of extravagance** – God set the standard first by extravagantly loving us through sending His Son. We are a people who by nature lavishly express our love to God. From a lower perspective, extravagant love looks wasteful; but we see from heaven's perspective.

Giving God Something to Work With

- **Schedule time to minister to Jesus** in prayer and worship.
- **Regularly find ways to be "excessively" generous**, and don't forget to give extravagantly to your own family.
- **Meditate on this story** in your time with God.

Declarations to Create Higher Perspectives

I am an extreme lover.

My giving is love driven, not guilt driven.

I regularly have extravagant love encounters with Jesus.

13 do not neglect the gift that is in you

In 1 Timothy, Paul instructs Timothy, his spiritual son, about living and leading. As he does, he makes an insightful reference concerning a gift Timothy has. *"Till I come, give attention to reading, to exhortation, to doctrine. **Do not neglect the gift that is in you, which was given to you by prophecy with the laying on of the hands of the eldership.** Meditate on these things; give yourself entirely to them, that your progress may be evident to all"* (1 Timothy 4:13-15). Paul added these words later, *"Therefore I remind you to stir up the gift of God which is in you through the laying on of my hands"* (2 Timothy 1:6).

Lower Perspectives

Paul could have concluded:

- Impartation is an out-dated, religious act for people who don't have the full revelation of what you receive at salvation.

- The purpose of prophecy is to predict the future, not to help release gifts in people.

- The laying on of hands is only for commissioning people into ministry.

- If a gift was not operating in Timothy, then it meant Timothy did not have that gift.

- The lack of a spiritual gift operating in us results from God's sovereignty, not our neglect of it.

Elevating Truths

1. **The gifts in us must be activated** – All Christians have the Holy Spirit in them, but the book of Acts reveals the need for being baptized in the Holy Spirit or being "filled" by the Spirit. This shows it is not automatic to walk in the Spirit's fullness.

Therefore, we are to believe for and pursue key moments of Holy Spirit activation for our gifts to flow.

2. **Leaders supernaturally release people into their fullness** – It's powerful when "elderships" believe that prophecy and the laying on of hands actually increase the gifts that will operate in those they minister to.

3. **We can stir up into operation what is in us** – Atrophy is physical weakness that occurs in muscles because of a lack of use. Spiritual atrophy happens when a gift in us is not used. We may feel extremely weak in a gift, but it (like a muscle) will get stronger as we use it.

Giving God Something to Work With

- **Thank God now** that past impartations you have received are still working in you.

- **Prophesy by speaking directly** to a person's destiny.

- **Exercise a gift in your life** that has been dormant.

Declarations to Create Higher Perspectives

I stir up the gifts in me.

I receive easily when leaders lay hands on me and prophesy over me.

All spiritual gifts are available to me.

14 and I will be even more undignified than this

*"Now as the ark of the LORD came into the City of David, Michal, Saul's daughter, looked through a window and saw King David leaping and whirling before the LORD; and she despised him in her heart ...And Michal ...said, 'How glorious was the king of Israel today, uncovering himself today in the eyes of the maids of his servants, as one of the base fellows shamelessly uncovers himself!' So David said to Michal, 'It was before the LORD, who chose me instead of your father and all his house, to appoint me ruler over the people of the LORD, over Israel. Therefore I will play music before the LORD. **And I will be even more undignified than this,** and will be humble in my own sight' ...Therefore Michal the daughter of Saul had no children to the day of her death."*

2 Samuel 6:16-23

Lower Perspectives

David could have concluded:

- Leaders are supposed to be dignified and unemotional about God.
- Pleasing Michal was more important than pleasing God.
- Dancing is for women, and he should go back to doing manly things.
- He should conform his behavior to what others think he should do.
- Dancing and whirling is charismatic emotionalism that only happens in the lives of unhinged, unstable simpletons who do not value scripture.

Elevating Truths

1. **Joyful celebration is vital in worship** – "Let the saints be joyful in glory; let them sing aloud on their beds. Let the high praises of God be in their mouth" (Psalm 149:5-6). "Praise Him with the

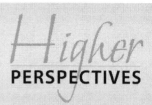
timbrel and dance ...Let everything that has breath praise the LORD" (Psalm 150:4-6).

2. **Rejoicing with those who rejoice releases life** – Michal, like the elder brother in Luke 15, was critical, jealous and cynical; and it adversely affected her life. Her supposed discernment of David's motives was warped due to her own unresolved issues. Healthy, fruitful people give others the benefit of the doubt and are enthusiastic in their own worship.

3. **Passion creates life** – Just as in the natural, life cannot be produced without passion, so it is in the spiritual. David understood this and gives us a wonderful example for us to follow. Let's join him on a never-ending pursuit to increase our passion for God.

Giving God Something to Work With

- **Prioritize corporate times of worship.**
- **Find ways to increase joy** and celebration in worship.
- **Overcome the critical spirit** by giving passionate people the benefit of the doubt.

Declarations to Create Higher Perspectives

I am going to new levels of passion in my worship.

I celebrate Jesus joyfully with others.

My passion creates life.

yet what I shall choose,
to live or to die

*"For to me, to live is Christ, and to die is gain. But if I live on in the flesh, this will mean fruit from my labor; **yet what I shall choose** I cannot tell. For I am hard-pressed between the two, having a desire to depart and be with Christ, which is far better. Nevertheless to remain in the flesh is more needful for you. And being confident of this, I know that I shall remain and continue with you all for your progress and joy of faith."*

Philippians 1:21-25

Lower Perspectives

Paul could have concluded:

- God has pre-ordained a time for everyone to die.

- God is totally uninterested in any desire we have because all our desires are evil.

- Getting to heaven as soon as possible is the most important thing.

- He could not have made a significant difference anyway, so it would be best that he went to heaven quickly.

Elevating Truths

1. **God partners with the desires of those who delight in Him** – "Delight yourself also in the LORD, and He shall give you the desires of your heart" (Psalm 37:4). As we move from a slave mentality to being a son, we will really hear John 15:7. "If you abide in Me, and My words abide in you, you will ask what you desire, and it shall be done for you."

2. **Our beliefs and core values greatly influence the length and quality of our lives** – "Keep my commands; for length of days and long life and peace they will add to you" (Proverbs 3:1-2). Jesus kept the commandments perfectly for us. As we believe

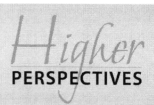

the truth, the benefit of a blessed, long life is increased. This is reinforced in Ephesians 6:2-3. "'Honor your father and mother,' which is the first commandment with promise: 'that it may be well with you and you may live long on the earth.'"

3. **Knowing our purpose enables us to really live** – Paul said, "Nevertheless to remain in the flesh is more needful for you. I shall remain and continue with you all for your progress and joy of faith." Provision for life comes from having a heavenly purpose. (See Matthew 6:33.) In many ways, we cease living when we stop believing we are significant.

Giving God Something to Work With

- **Dedicate your life** to see others strong in Christ.
- **Walk in honor** in every situation.
- **Choose to give time to discipling** a new believer or to evangelize.

Declarations to Create Higher Perspectives

My purpose in life is to know Jesus and make Him known.

My descendants and I live long, influential lives.

I am a powerful evangelist.

"And God said to Noah... 'Make yourself an ark... I Myself am bringing flood-waters on the earth, to destroy from under heaven all flesh in which is the breath of life; everything that is on the earth shall die. But I will establish My covenant with you; and you shall go into the ark - you, your sons, your wife, and your sons' wives with you. And of every living thing of all flesh you shall bring two of every sort into the ark, to keep them alive with you... ***Thus Noah did; according to all that God commanded him, so he did.***

Genesis 6:13-22

Lower Perspectives

Noah could have concluded:

- If it has never happened in the past, it cannot happen in the future.

- If a direction is illogical, then it cannot be from God.

- Blending in with the community will pay off in the long run more than partnering with the voice of God.

- Since the whole earth is being flooded, he should not trust God concerning his own family.

- God has assigned him an unrealistic task and would not give him the resources to fulfill it.

- This will be impossible since he cannot get his own pets to obey him.

Elevating Truths

1. **We are equipped for our calling** – God never asks us to do something without equipping us to accomplish it. 2 Peter 1:3 says, "His divine power has given to us all things that pertain to life and godliness..." We are specifically designed to succeed in all that comes our way.

2. **Faith is rooted in the unseen** – Sometimes it can become routine to apply faith in areas we have seen before. Hebrews 11:1 tells us that faith is "the substance of things hoped for, the evidence of things not seen." We live by faith, not by sight (2 Corinthians 5:7). As believers, we thrive in the unseen.

3. **God is the God of the impossible** – When the disciples were trying to identify the ghost-like figure walking on the water, Peter's one test was, "Lord, if it is You, command me to come to You on the water" (Matthew 14:28). God is known for inviting us into the impossible.

Giving God Something to Work With

- **Make a practical step towards a dream that seems impossible.**
- **Pray for something you've never seen happen before.**
- **Make a long-term decision that plans for the future.**

Declarations to Create Higher Perspectives

I have faith in seemingly impossible situations.

I am equipped for my calling and destiny.

I make good decisions that propel me into my destiny.

17 shout for the Lord has given you the city

"But it came to pass on the seventh day that they rose early... and marched around the city seven times in the same manner. On that day only they marched around the city seven times. And the seventh time it happened, when the priests blew the trumpets, that Joshua said to the people: 'Shout, for the Lord has given you the city!'... And it happened when the people heard the sound of the trumpet, and the people shouted with a great shout, that the wall fell down flat. Then the people went up into the city, every man straight before him, and they took the city."

Joshua 6:15-20

Lower Perspectives

Joshua could have concluded:

- Prophetic acts are only symbolic and have no physical effect.

- God would never use a creative, unorthodox battle plan.

- They should wait for the walls to start crumbling before shouting.

- They should have a back-up plan ready with more men and better weapons because this was likely not to work.

- This was probably a test from God, and He would be more pleased if they circled the city 10 or 15 times instead of only seven.

- Joshua should not make this bold of a declaration because maybe nothing would happen.

Elevating Truths

1. **Prophetic acts are powerful** – All through the Old and New Testament, God instructed His people to do prophetic acts that brought a dramatic shift to the circumstance. In 2 Corinthians 10:3 it says, "For though we walk according to the

flesh, we do not war according to the flesh." Often the real battle isn't what we see in front of us; the battle is in the spiritual realm.

2. **God will only lead you into battles He has positioned you to win** – There isn't a single story in Scripture where God sends His people into battle, and did not give them a strategy to win. Just like an earthly father wants to watch his kids succeed in life, how much more would God position His children for victory?

3. **Revelation of what we already have in Christ will bring the shout of victory** – Romans 8:37 tells us that we are "more than conquerors." Believing we are victorious is often the most important part of the battle. The essence of faith is to believe something is ours before we have actually experienced it. Let's believe now that we are victorious in Christ!

Giving God Something to Work With

- **Lead a group of people** in a prophetic act.
- **Approach an obstacle** with a creative solution.
- **Make a bold declaration** over a seemingly impossible situation in your life.
- **Speak up** in a group of people with a bold declaration.

Declarations to Create Higher Perspectives

I am positioned for victory.

My prophetic acts shift circumstances.

My faith declarations demolish strongholds.

18 but only speak a word, and my servant will be healed

"Now when Jesus had entered Capernaum, a centurion came to Him, pleading with Him, saying, 'Lord, my servant is lying at home paralyzed, dreadfully tormented.' And Jesus said to him, 'I will come and heal him.' The centurion answered and said, 'Lord I am not worthy that You should come under my roof. **But only speak a word, and my servant will be healed.'***... When Jesus heard it, He marveled, and said to those who followed, 'Assuredly, I say to you, I have not found such great faith, not even in Israel!'... Then Jesus said to the centurion, 'Go your way; and as you have believed, so let it be done for you.' And his servant was healed that same hour."*

Matthew 8:5-13

Lower Perspectives

The Centurion could have concluded:

- It is unwise to make assumptions about Jesus' power or authority unless you have seen Jesus do it before.

- He shouldn't have put Jesus "on the spot" in front of a crowd. Jesus will probably rebuke him for potentially embarrassing Him.

- Jesus would not answer his request because He only heals Christians.

- Healing only comes when we go to the sick and lay hands on them, and anoint them with oil.

- Spoken words alone cannot bring breakthrough or transformation.

Elevating Truths

1. **Life is in the power of the tongue** – Creation was set into motion as God spoke. This was not just a display of His power, but an invitation for us to follow. We carry life and our tongue is a portal for the kingdom to be released.

2. **The unsaved are targets for miracles** – "For God so loved the world that He gave His only begotten Son..." (John 3:16). He radically loves the whole world. God is in the business of reconciling the world back to Himself through love. We have been commissioned into the same vision. One of the many ways love beautifully manifests is through miracles and healing. The lost carry a bulls-eye for radical God encounters.

3. **Nothing is impossible** – In the gospels, Jesus repeatedly astounded onlookers by healing the sick, exercising authority over the elements and defying the laws of physics. He showed us that nothing was impossible and then empowered us into the same work: "The works that I do he will do also; and greater works than these he will do" (John 14:12).

Giving God Something to Work With

- **Try pursuing healing** through declarations and blessings.
- **Write down some initial steps** towards pursuing an "impossible" dream.
- **Pray for a miracle** you've never seen before.

Declarations to Create Higher Perspectives

My words are powerful.

The unsaved constantly experience miracles through me.

Nothing is impossible for me.

let it be to me
according to your word

*"And the angel answered and said to her, 'The Holy Spirit will come upon you, and the power of the Highest will overshadow you; therefore, also, that Holy One who is to be born will be called the Son of God. Now indeed, Elizabeth your relative has also conceived a son in her old age; and this is now the sixth month for her who was called barren. **For with God nothing will be impossible.'** Then Mary said, 'Behold the maidservant of the Lord! **Let it be to me according to your word.'** And the angel departed from her."*

Luke 1:35-38

Lower Perspectives

Mary could have concluded:

- God does not need our cooperation to accomplish His will on earth.

- Surrendering to God's purposes will ruin her life.

- God does not use young women to do great things.

- Miraculous things happened in the past but won't happen now.

- God's word won't empower her to do the impossible, so it will be all up to her to make it happen.

Elevating Truths

1. **Surrendering to God makes us spiritually fertile to conceive the "impossible"** – Isaiah "heard the voice of the Lord, saying: 'Whom shall I send, and who will go for Us?' Then he said, 'Here am I! Send me'" (Isaiah 6:8). When we receive God's heart and purposes for our life, we will become a part of miraculous interventions on planet earth.

2. **God's spoken promise to us contains the power to make it happen** – Our faith is not to be in our ability to do something, but in the power of the words spoken to us. Jesus said, "The

words that I speak to you are spirit, and they are life" (John 6:63). Scripture also says that good words "impart grace to the hearers" (Ephesians 4:29). Grace is *the empowerment to do God's will.* When God speaks direction to us, His words literally will empower us to accomplish what He has said.

3. **God partners with unlikely people for the miraculous** – Mary was young, female, and put in a situation where her reputation was questioned, but she was used in an incredible way – so can we be used.

Giving God Something to Work With

- **As a regular part of your corporate worship times**, surrender your life in a fresh way to God.

- **Speak scriptural promises over your life** and believe the Word is empowering you.

- **Find ways to work with God** instead of working for God.

Declarations to Create Higher Perspectives

I live my life for the glory of God.

Great things are ahead for me in my life.

The miraculous is birthed in me and through me.

20 greater works than these you will do

*"Most assuredly, I say to you, he who believes in Me, the works that I do he will do also; and **greater works than these he will do**, because I go to My Father. And whatever you ask in My name, that I will do" (John 14:12-13).* Jesus states an almost unbelievable promise to those who believe that they will do greater things than He did. This truth takes all limits off of our potential.

Lower Perspectives

We could have concluded:

- Jesus was only speaking metaphorically when He said we would do greater things than Him.

- The experiences that Christians have had in the past are all we can expect in the future.

- Pursuing greater things is unnecessary and possibly evil. We should wait for God to sovereignly bless us with them in the time He selects.

- Jesus was referring to all Christians together doing greater things, not one person.

Elevating Truths

1. **The reformation is still continuing** – Martin Luther started what is known as The Reformation on October 31, 1517, by nailing the *95 Theses* to the door of the Castle Church in Wittenberg, Germany. He had revelation of truths in Scripture that were not being taught. There is still more revelation coming, including the mighty acts and influence (the greater things) that one person full of the Holy Spirit can do.

2. **Believing is powerful** – Jesus said, "All things are possible to

him who believes" (Mark 9:23). When Mary wondered how the "impossible" could be done, the angel told her, "For with God nothing will be impossible" (Luke 1:37). In the same way, Jesus said, "If you have faith as a mustard seed... nothing will be impossible for you" (Matthew 17:20).

3. **Desire more of the Holy Spirit to manifest in your life** – Listen to what Jesus said, "If you then, being evil, know how to give good gifts to your children, how much more will your heavenly Father give the Holy Spirit to those who ask Him!" (Luke 11:13).

Giving God Something to Work With

- **Build relationships with those operating in signs and wonders.**

- **Consume testimonies of healings, miracles, and dramatic conversions.**

- **Devour the Gospels and the book of Acts.**

Declarations to Create Higher Perspectives

Because Jesus went to the Father, I do even greater things than He did.

Signs and wonders follow me wherever I go.

The potential for my life is unlimited.

21

and he
laid him on the altar

"Now it came to pass... that God tested Abraham, and said to him, 'Abraham!... Take now your son... and offer him there as a burnt offering'... And Abraham built an altar there and placed the wood in order; and **he bound Isaac his son and laid him on the altar,** *upon the wood. And Abraham stretched out his hand and took the knife to slay his son. But the Angel of the Lord called to him from heaven and said... 'Do not lay your hand on the lad... for now I know that you fear God, since you have not withheld your son, your only son, from Me."*

Genesis 22:1-12

Lower Perspectives

Abraham could have concluded:

- He missed God's voice somewhere, because God will never change what He says.

- God gets deep gratification from seeing us sacrifice things we love.

- We should never get attached to anything because God will always rip it out of our hands. He enjoys seeing us miserable.

- If we don't understand God's ways, it is better to just ignore Him.

Elevating Truths

1. **If God asks us to give something up, it is for our benefit** – There are two primary things God would ask us to surrender: a habit that is destroying us or hurting others, and an affection or belief that is blocking our destiny. Because Abraham was going to higher places in life, it was important for him to pass the test of loving the promise giver more than the promise.

2. **God's goodness is not dependent on our understanding** – Isaiah 55:9 says, "For as the heavens are higher than the earth, So

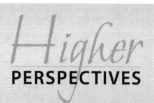

are My ways higher than your ways, And My thoughts than your thoughts." It is crucial for believers to learn that God is good, regardless of our circumstances. We believe in God's goodness even when we can't see it.

3. **Life comes through God's proceeding word** – Jesus said, "Man shall not live by bread alone, but by every word that proceeds from the mouth of God" (Matthew 4:4). God is constantly speaking, and if we only focus on what He has said, we will miss what He is saying. Staying connected to His voice causes us to experience and release life.

Giving God Something to Work With

- **Trust God** in a confusing situation.
- **Trust God with something valuable** to you.
- **Trust the proceeding word** over difficult circumstances.

Declarations to Create Higher Perspectives

I trust God's goodness, especially in confusing times.

Obedience positions me for blessing.

*I willingly give up habits that are hindrances
to the promises of God over my life.*

22   oh that You would bless me indeed

*"Now Jabez was more honorable than his brothers, and his mother called his name Jabez, saying, 'Because I bore him in pain.' And Jabez called on the God of Israel saying, **'Oh, that You would bless me indeed,** and enlarge my territory, that Your hand would be with me, and that You would keep me from evil, that I may not cause pain!' So God granted him what he requested"* (1 Chronicles 4:9-10). The circumstances surrounding Jabez's birth led his mother to give him a name that means *I gave birth to him in pain.* In biblical times, names were often prophetic toward the child's future. Jabez overcame these words and received a life contrary to pain by believing God was good and boldly asking to be blessed.

Lower Perspectives

Jabez could have concluded:

- Because of his name, God had predestined him to a life of pain and toil.

- He would never have favor because even his mother did not like him.

- He would never bring anything but pain to others.

- He was just an inconvenience and shouldn't even be alive.

- His past experience would define his future.

Elevating Truths

1. **We have a good Father who longs to bless us** – "If you then, being evil, know how to give good gifts to your children, how much more will your Father in heaven give good gifts to those who ask Him!" (Matthew 7:11). Loving parents desire to see their children happy and blessed.

2. **We can break free of constraints on our lives** – Jabez broke free of word curses and the false perceptions of him. We also are overcomers because, in Jesus, we are "more than conquerors" (Romans 8:37).

3. **Jesus came that we may have an abundant and victorious life** – "The thief does not come except to steal, and to kill, and to destroy. I have come that they may have life, and that they may have it more abundantly" (John 10:10). We have victory over curses, intimidation, doubt and fear through the blood of Jesus.

Giving God Something to Work With

- **Identify areas of your life** where you believe other's words are more powerful than God's blessings.
- **Speak blessings over your life** and those around you.
- **Trust that God is an incredibly good Father** who has amazing things for you.

Declarations to Create Higher Perspectives

I attract the blessings and favor of God.

My influence is growing every day.

Those around me are blessed by the blessing on my life.

she did according to the word of Elijah

"(Elijah) called to her (the widow) and said, 'Please bring me a little water in a cup'... And as she was going to get it, he called to her and said, 'Please bring me a morsel of bread in your hand.' So she said, '... I do not have bread, only a handful of flour in a bin, and a little oil in a jar'... And Elijah said to her, 'Do not fear; go and do as you have said, but make me a small cake from it first, and bring it to me and afterward make some for yourself and your son. For thus says the Lord God of Israel: "The bin of flour shall not be used up, nor shall the jar of oil run dry"'... So she... did according to the word of Elijah; and she and he and her household ate for many days."

I Kings 17:10-15

Lower Perspectives

The widow could have concluded:

- Generosity is only for wealthy people and is never sacrificial.

- Reaping a return only works with the church tithe model.

- Because she didn't instantly display faith, God would only make enough food for Elijah thus punishing her family.

- She should not give Elijah anything because, scripturally, he should be looking after orphans and widows, not asking for food from them.

- If Elijah was really a man of God, he should never have to ask other people for anything.

Elevating Truths

1. **Extreme generosity leads to extreme blessing** – While we never want to slip into a striving or works mentality, we can be encouraged by understanding the limitless biblical principle of sowing and reaping. In Luke 6:38, Jesus references giving saying, "For with the same measure that you use, it will be measured back to you." You can't out-give God.

2. **God does miracles through unlikely people** – Instead of searching for a wealthy person, Elijah asks a poor, hungry widow for food. He learned that God uses even the most unlikely people to release the supernatural. With God, a good place to expect is in the place where you least expect Him to show up.

3. **Relationship releases breakthrough** – Elijah had the faith, and the widow had the food, but without each other, both were in lack. When they were able to come together, God released breakthrough that blessed everyone. Needing people is a strength, not a weakness.

Giving God Something to Work With

- **Give sacrificially** to someone.
- **Pray for a miracle to be released** through you in an area where you feel unqualified.
- **Ask someone for help** in an area of weakness.

Declarations to Create Higher Perspectives

I joyfully search out opportunities to be generous.

Breakthrough is released through my relationships.

I welcome people into my life who strengthen me.

24 so I prophesied and they came to life

Ezekiel partners his words with the Holy Spirit and brings supernatural life to dry bones. *"The hand of the LORD came upon me and brought me out in the Spirit of the LORD, and set me down in the midst of the valley; and it was full of bones... He said to me, 'Prophesy to these bones, and say to them, "O dry bones, hear the word of the Lord! Thus says the Lord God to these bones: 'Surely I will cause breath to enter into you, and you shall live.'"'... So I prophesied... and breath came into them, and they lived, and stood upon their feet, an exceedingly great army."*

Ezekiel 37:1-10

Lower Perspectives

Ezekiel could have concluded:

- Some situations are just too impossible, even for God.

- His words did not carry enough power to bring life back to dead places or people.

- The people's sins and rebellion were too great and cut them off from God with no hope of restoration.

- The purpose of prophetic ministry is to diagnose the past experience of people or places, not to release transforming words.

Elevating Truths

1. **We have the power to create life with our words** – "Death and life are in the power of the tongue. And those who love it will eat its fruit" (Proverbs 18:21). Our words are our most powerful tool in releasing breakthrough and supernatural life into situations.

2. **There are no impossible situations** – "Jesus said to him (the man with the demon possessed son), all things are possible to him who believes" (Mark 9:23). Every time we declare 'He can' to

our situation, it releases His life-giving power for breakthrough.

3. **We can expect to live a supernatural life** – When we partner our beliefs, words, and actions with the Creator of everything, this partnership will produce supernatural breakthrough and life. "These signs will follow those who believe" (Mark 16:17).

Giving God Something to Work With

- **Increase your speaking** TO things in prayer (study the gospels and Acts for examples of this).
- **Ask God** how He sees "dead" areas in your life.
- **Read Steve Backlund's book** *You're Crazy If You Don't Talk to Yourself.*

Declarations to Create Higher Perspectives

My words bring life to impossible situations.

I carry the DNA of Christ, so WHEN I speak, circumstances shift.

I release God's goodness to other people daily through my words.

*"I press on, that I may lay hold of that for which Christ Jesus has also laid hold of me. Brethren, I do not count myself to have apprehended; but one thing I do, **forgetting those things which are behind and reaching forward to those things which are ahead,** I press toward the goal for the prize of the upward call of God in Christ Jesus."*

Philippians 3:12-14

Lower Perspectives

Paul could have concluded:

- His past disqualified him from God's best in the future.

- The purpose of his memory was to focus on his mistakes so they would not happen again.

- There are no greater things in the future for someone like him.

- Vision for the future does not give power for the present.

- Continually trying to fix his past will bring lasting change in his life.

Elevating Truths

1. **Past happenings are not as big a problem as our current beliefs** – No one's past can stop them from God's best, but current beliefs can. Paul's regrets for being a persecutor of Christians would seem difficult to overcome, but he did. We too can overcome shame and regret.

2. **We have permission to forget that which needs to be forgotten** – Philippians 4:8 and 2 Corinthians 10:5 reveal that we are empowered to think intentionally. We can supernaturally forget events of the past, as well as, the conclusions we made about ourselves from those experiences. We can think on purpose by taking thoughts captive and declaring what God

says about our past and us.

3. **Focusing on "the things ahead" will build a wall against negatively dwelling on the past** – Ephesians 4:22-32 teaches us that one key for putting off the wrong is to put on the right. It won't work to just try to stop negative thoughts. Destructive thinking easily returns where there is not a positive belief system present. A key to overcoming regret is to be future-focused and dwell on "those things that are ahead" in our lives.

Giving God Something to Work With

- **Ask God for a revelation** of the depth of His forgiveness.

- **Get healing ministry** for the hurts of the past so that your conclusions about your identity line up with God's word.

- **Frequently review the promises and prophecies** that God has made real to you.

Declarations to Create Higher Perspectives

I have an unusual ability to overcome regret and shame.

Great things are ahead for me in my life.

I think on purpose and have vision for the future.

26 Lord, if it is You, command me to come

*"And when the disciples saw Him (Jesus) walking on the sea, they were troubled, saying, 'It is a ghost!' And they cried out for fear. But immediately Jesus spoke to them, saying, 'Be of good cheer! It is I; do not be afraid.' And Peter answered Him and said, **'Lord, if it is You, command me to come to You on the water.'** So He said, 'Come.' And when Peter had come down out of the boat, he walked on the water to go to Jesus" (Matthew 14:26-29). Peter overcame the spirit of fear that was on the boat and had a barrier-breaking spiritual experience."*

Lower Perspectives

Peter could have concluded:

- He should wait until Jesus told him what to do.
- Miracles like walking on water ceased with Elijah and the prophets.
- He could not walk on water because that is scientifically impossible.
- He should do what the other disciples were doing in the boat so that they would not think he was showing off.
- He was becoming too heavenly-minded to be of any earthly good.

Elevating Truths

1. **Nothing is impossible** – The man with the demonized son said to Jesus, "If You can do anything... help us." Jesus said to him, "If you can believe, all things are possible to him who believes" (Mark 9:22-23). The question isn't just if God can do something, but more importantly it is how much we can believe for.

2. **Anything Jesus does, we can do** – Just as a toddler intuitively

knows that he can do what his parents do, Peter understood that Jesus was setting an example of higher ways to live. "Most assuredly, I say to you, he who believes in Me, the works that I do he will do also; and greater works than these he will do, because I go to My Father" (John 14:12).

3. **Spiritual experimentation is needed for advancement to occur** – Someone has to do something that has never been done before. Just as in the natural, Spiritual progress will not occur unless a person is dissatisfied with the status quo and seeks a higher way of living in the Lord.

Giving God Something to Work With

* **Do something spiritually** that you have never heard anyone else do, for example, in Acts 19 a handkerchief healed the sick.

* **Ask God to see miracles** in your life.

* **Feast on testimonies** of people who have had supernatural experiences in the Lord.

Declarations to Create Higher Perspectives

I seize special moments in the Lord to participate in the miraculous.

Jesus says "come" to me, so I come.

I encounter the Lord in supernatural ways.

...fill up the water pots with water

*"The mother of Jesus said to Him, 'They have no wine.' Jesus said to her, 'Woman, what does your concern have to do with Me? My hour has not yet come.' His mother said to the servants, 'Whatever He says to you, do it.' Now there were set there six water pots of stone... containing twenty or thirty gallons apiece. **Jesus said to them, 'Fill the water pots with water.'** And they filled them up to the brim. And He said to them, 'Draw some out now, and take it to the master of the feast.'... And he said to (the bridegroom), 'Every man at the beginning sets out the good wine, and when the guests have well drunk, then the inferior. You have kept the good wine until now!'"*

John 2:3-10

Lower Perspectives

The servants could have concluded:

- If Jesus was going to do a miracle, He would not want or need anything from them to be a catalyst in making it happen.

- Jesus' request does not make sense, so it could not be from God.

- Miracles only happen in far away countries.

- Miracles are only for clearly spiritual purposes, and this does not fit into that category.

- They were spiritually unqualified to participate in a miracle.

Elevating Truths

1. **We need to be open to releasing a miracle in a surprising situation** – Jesus didn't begin to lecture and condemn the sin of the drunk people at this wedding. He created more wine. Miracles exist to point towards the goodness, extravagance, and mercy of God rather than a set of rules.

2. **Miracles increase dramatically if God has something to work with** – A tree thrown into bitter water made the waters sweet

(Exodus 15:22-27). Two fish and five loaves were used to feed a multitude (Matthew 14:17-21). An arrow striking the ground determined future levels of national victory (2 Kings 13:18-19). The number of containers available determined the amount of oil for the widow (2 Kings 4:1-7).

3. **Risk-takers see more miracles** – Consider these miracles:

   - **Peter** walking on water (Matthew 14:22-33)

   - **Bartimaeus** receiving his sight (Mark 10:46-52)

   - **Peter and John** bringing healing to the lame man (Acts 3:1-10)

   - **Hebrew children** receiving ten times greater wisdom (Daniel 1:8-20)

All these risked failure before the miracle happened.

Giving God Something to Work With

- **Take at least one risk** every day to increase the likelihood that God will do something powerful.

- **Study the details behind extraordinary miracles.**

- **Be ready** to participate in non-conventional steps to see a miracle happen.

Declarations to Create Higher Perspectives

I cause great spiritual things to happen.

When I take risks, heaven responds.

I activate angelic activity.

how will the ministry of the Spirit not be more glorious?

*"But if the ministry of death, written and engraved on stones, was glorious, so that the children of Israel could not look steadily at the face of Moses because of the glory of his countenance, which glory was passing away, **how will the ministry of the Spirit not be more glorious?** For if the ministry of condemnation had glory, the ministry of righteousness exceeds much more in glory. For even what was made glorious had no glory in this respect, because of the glory that excels. For if what is passing away was glorious, what remains is much more glorious."*

2 Corinthians 3:7-11

Lower Perspectives

Paul could have concluded:

- Moses had already experienced the pinnacle of all "God encounters."

- The further removed from biblical times, the less glory is available.

- Moses was a rare blip on the radar, so he should not get his hopes up for experiencing God's glory.

- Having the Holy Spirit "in him" sounds more powerful than it really is.

- At best, he could hope for a similar experience as Moses, but even then, he would probably be exaggerating.

Elevating Truths

1. **We are gaining a "glory momentum"** – As believers, it is foundational to understand that we are moving from glory to glory (2 Corinthians 3:18). When Jesus gave us the Holy Spirit, that was a greater glory. We, ministering in the Spirit, continue advancing from glory to glory!

2. **We carry an even greater glory than Moses did** – Moses was an example of what was available to mankind before the cross. Jesus paid for the restoration of perfect union with God and the indwelling of the Holy Spirit. What we now have access to far surpasses the greatest of Old Testament experiences.

3. **God saves the best wine for last** – The Kingdom of God continues to advance, and revival is spreading around the world. We, as believers, draw encouragement from the realization that spiritual momentum increases the farther in time from the cross we get.

Giving God Something to Work With

- **Re-read 2 Corinthians 3.** Soak in its truths and ask God for fresh revelation from this chapter.

- **Meditate on the truth** that the glory you carry is greater than what Moses experienced.

- **Make room in your life,** and in any meetings you lead, for the glory to manifest.

Declarations to Create Higher Perspectives

I walk in the ministry of the Holy Spirit.

I move from glory to glory.

Daily I am tapping into a 2000-year glory momentum.

as the Lord lives...
I will not leave you!

*"When the LORD was about to take up Elijah into heaven... Elijah said to (Elisha), 'Stay here, please, for the LORD has sent me on... ' But (Elisha) said, **'As the LORD lives,** and as your soul lives, **I will not leave you!'...** And so... Elijah said to Elisha, 'Ask! What may I do for you, before I am taken away from you?' Elisha said, 'Please let a double portion of your spirit be upon me.' So he said... 'If you see me when I am taken from you, it shall be so for you... ' Then... suddenly a chariot of fire appeared... and Elijah went up by a whirlwind into heaven... (Elisha) took the mantle of Elijah... (The prophets) said, "The spirit of Elijah rests on Elisha."*

2 Kings 2:1-15

Lower Perspectives

Elisha could have concluded:

- He was a victim of abandonment and should give up all hope that he could complete his training or reach his full potential.

- He was unworthy of greater supernatural experiences because his leader did not invite him along.

- God loved Elijah more than him because he got a bigger promotion.

- Desiring what Elijah carried would be coveting and wanting twice as much could only result from a greedy and arrogant spirit.

Elevating Truths

1. **Follow your heart against all odds** – Elisha overcame pressure from his friends to stay behind and pursued the higher course until the end. "Forgetting those things which are behind and reaching forward to those things which are ahead, I press toward the goal for the prize of the upward call of God in Christ Jesus" (Philippians 3:13-14).

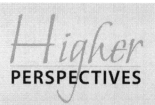
2. **Serving leaders positions us for impartation** – Elisha gave his life to serve Elijah; in turn he received a double portion of his anointing, leading to twice as many miracles. "He who receives a prophet in the name of a prophet shall receive a prophet's reward" (Matthew 10:41).

3. **Tenacious faith has great reward** – "He who comes to God must believe that He is, and that He is a rewarder of those who diligently seek Him" (Hebrews 11:6). "The kingdom of heaven suffers violence, and the violent take it by force" (Matthew 11:12).

Giving God Something to Work With

- **Discover and list your dreams** that are bigger than yourself.
- **Partner with people "stronger" than you** and serve them.
- **Don't give up too easily** on the important relationships in your life.

Declarations to Create Higher Perspectives

I have a servant's heart, and I have great influence in the Kingdom of Heaven.

There is nothing that can hold me back as I lay hold of my destiny.

I carry a double-portion anointing.

30 then Jonathan and David made a covenant

*"Now when he had finished speaking to Saul, the soul of Jonathan was knit to the soul of David, and Jonathan loved him as his own soul. Saul took him that day, and would not let him go home to his father's house anymore. **Then Jonathan and David made a covenant,** because he loved him as his own soul. And Jonathan took off the robe that was on him and gave it to David, with his armor, even to his sword and his bow and his belt"* (1 Samuel 18:1-4). Jonathan was the logical successor to his father, King Saul, but God chose David instead of him to be the next king. After he understood this, Jonathan displayed a very high perspective in his response to David and other's expectations.

Lower Perspectives

Jonathan could have concluded:

- He should be jealous of David and see him as his biggest life problem.

- Being anything less than king would be a second-class calling.

- Deep heart connections with others are a waste of time.

- He should dig up dirt on David's past and release it to the media.

- Children are a failure if they do not meet their parents' expectations.

- He should be more concerned about his own success than national success.

Elevating Truths

1. **Becoming someone great is more important than having a great position** – Jonathan saw a perspective and lifestyle in David that was more important than his own worldly success. He determined to pursue personal growth more than positional

promotion.

2. **Healthy relationships are the foundation to extraordinary leadership** – We are not a leader because we have a good message, but because we have a life that others want to follow. When we prioritize healthy relationships above successful ministry, then we will actually hasten our progress toward becoming a true leader.

3. **The sons of Issachar represent who we are to become** – "The sons of Issachar... had understanding of the times, to know what Israel ought to do" (1 Chronicles 12:32). Jonathan saw that God's hand was on David; therefore, he gave himself to something higher than his own temporal success. We too can walk in this kind of spiritual discernment.

Giving God Something to Work With

- **Generously support someone** who seems like a competitor of yours.
- **Ask God for a specific step to increase** your heart connections with others and do it.
- **Do a study** on covenant relationships.

Declarations to Create Higher Perspectives

I have healthy, long-term relationships.

I am more concerned about God's kingdom than my own.

31

stand still, and see the salvation of the Lord

*"And the LORD hardened the heart of Pharaoh king of Egypt, and he pursued the children of Israel; and the children of Israel went out with boldness. So the Egyptians pursued them, all the horses and chariots of Pharaoh... and overtook them... the children of Israel lifted their eyes, and... they were very afraid... And Moses said to the people, "Do not be afraid. **Stand still, and see the salvation of the Lord,** which He will accomplish for you today. For the Egyptians whom you see today, you shall see again no more forever. The Lord will fight for you, and you shall hold your peace."*

Exodus 14:8-14

Lower Perspectives

Moses could have concluded:

- Obedience honors God, but it would never lead to blessing in this life.

- He should draw his sword because God will never fight his battles.

- It is safer to go back to familiar things of the past than to trust God to lead him into his promises.

- A good leader would surrender in order to protect his people.

- This could be an opportunity to make a truce with Pharaoh because compromise is always better than commitment to something.

Elevating Truths

1. **Remembering God's faithfulness releases confidence into the present** – Our memory is a powerful force. While the enemy attempts to shift our focus on failures, God points us toward our past victories. A memory focused on failures releases fear and doubt, but a memory yielded to God's direction releases boldness. Choosing to remember His goodness empowers us

with confidence for the present.

2. **God's deliverance always leads to freedom** – Many times God's deliverance is a multi-step, exciting process. While the Israelites continued questioning God's deliverance, Moses knew that "He who has begun a good work in you will complete it... " (Philippians 1:6).

3. **"Being still" is being strong** – Ephesians 6:13 tells us that after putting on the full armor of God, our job is to stand. When we choose to be still and carry peace, God will crush Satan under our feet (Romans 16:20). We are powerful when we let Him be powerful.

Giving God Something to Work With

*   **Saturate yourself in testimonies** of personal past victories.
*   **Be proactive to schedule time** to be inactive and rest.
*   **Ask God to reveal an area of your life** that He can be strong for you.

Declarations to Create Higher Perspectives

I am a powerful force when I rest.

I have an unusual ability to draw strength from past victories.

I am being led into greater and greater freedom daily!

32 Lord, do not charge them with this sin

"He... gazed into heaven and saw the glory of God, and Je-sus standing at the right hand of God, and said, 'Look! I see the heavens opened and the Son of Man standing at the right hand of God!' Then they cried out with a loud voice, stopped their ears, and ran at him with one accord; and they cast him out of the city and stoned him. And the witnesses laid down their clothes at the feet of a young man named Saul. And they stoned Stephen as he was calling on God and saying, 'Lord Jesus, receive my spirit.' Then he knelt down and cried out with a loud voice, 'Lord, do not charge them with this sin.'"

Acts 7:55-60

Lower Perspectives

Stephen could have concluded:

- When he forgives others, nothing powerful happens in the spirit realm.
- Grace and forgiveness are only for a select and predestined few.
- He plays no part in the ministry of forgiveness of sins.
- Murder is an unpardonable sin.
- Intentional forgiveness is not a weapon that advances the kingdom.
- Sowing and reaping is a higher law than grace and forgiveness.

Elevating Truths

1. **Our forgiveness creates an open heaven over those we forgive** – Saul's dramatic conversion came shortly after Stephen's radical forgiveness. Similarly, Jesus forgiving the sins of mankind paved a way for Pentecost. There is deep power and breakthrough in forgiveness.

2. **God forgives people who don't deserve it** – Paul tells us in Ephesians 2:8-9, "For by grace you have been saved through faith, and that not of yourselves; it is the gift of God, not of works, lest anyone should boast." It is foundational for us, as believers, to understand that our sins being forgiven has nothing to do with what we've done and everything to do with what He did.

3. **Forgiving sins is a normal part of the Spirit-filled life** – In John 20:22-23, Jesus breathes on the disciples and gives them the Holy Spirit. His first words following are, "Receive the Holy Spirit. If you forgive the sins of any, they are forgiven them... " Astoundingly, Jesus passes us the baton and empowers us to carry on His ministry of forgiveness.

Giving God Something to Work With

- **Regularly stir up thankfulness** concerning your own salvation.
- **Ask God for His heart** about someone who has wronged you.
- **In prayer, declare forgiveness** over specific people or people groups.

Declarations to Create Higher Perspectives

My forgiveness is forerunning and positioning others for God encounters.

I see those who have wronged me through God's lens of grace and redemption.

I forgive others easily.

33 husbands, without a word, may be won

*"Wives, likewise, be submissive to your own **husbands**, that even if some do not obey the word, they, **without a word, may be won** by the conduct of their wives, when they observe your chaste conduct accompanied by fear. Do not let your adornment be merely outward—arranging the hair, wearing gold, or putting on fine apparel--rather let it be the hidden person of the heart, with the incorruptible beauty of a gentle and quiet spirit, which is very precious in the sight of God."*

1 Peter 3:1-4

Lower Perspectives

When we are not heard, we could conclude:

- If people are not hearing us, it is always their fault.

- He who talks the most and is the loudest has the most influence.

- We should be quick to speak, quick to anger and slow to listen.

- We can never expect to be heard by those in our family.

- There are no seasons in life where our primary goal is to build trust in the minds and hearts of others.

- The best way to influence others is to become angry with those who do not listen to us.

Elevating Truths

1. **A transformed life is our greatest message** – "You are our epistle written... read by all men" (2 Corinthians 3:2). People will want to hear more from those radically changed in Christ.

2. **Winning people to ourselves creates lasting influence** – Remember: An anointed person can create a great meeting, but a true leader can create a movement. Ultimately, we cannot lead unless we "win" people to the place where they determine we are trustworthy and have a lifestyle they want to follow.

3. **Our character speaks more than our words ever will** – We can increase other people's trust in us by walking in wisdom, by following through on what we say, admitting our mistakes, being thankful, loving others, walking in integrity and humility, taking interest in the lives of others, believing we have favor, and carry His presence wherever we go.

Giving God Something to Work With

- **Refuse to be discouraged** or angry when you are not heard.
- **Take a specific step in your life** that will cause people to trust you more.
- **Connect with someone** who does not value your voice.

Declarations to Create Higher Perspectives

Because of the way I live my life, people want to listen to me.

I have astounding influence in the lives of others.

I live a life of humility and great integrity.

34 the Lord forbid that I should stretch out my hand against the Lord's anointed

*David was told by God years earlier that he would be the next king of Israel. Saul, the current king was unpopular and irrational. David had an opportunity to kill Saul. "So David and Abishai came to the people by night; and there Saul lay sleeping within the camp... Then Abishai said to David, 'God has delivered your enemy into your hand this day. Now therefore, please, let me strike him at once with the spear... ' But David said to Abishai, 'Do not destroy him; for who can stretch out his hand against the LORD's anointed, and be guiltless?... As the LORD lives, the LORD shall strike him, or his day shall come to die, or he shall go out to battle and perish. **The LORD forbid that I should stretch out my hand against the LORD's anointed.**"*

1 Samuel 26:7-11

Lower Perspectives

David could have concluded:

- People standing in the way of his prophetic destiny were his enemies.

- God brought Saul before him to be killed, not as a test of his heart.

- Time is ticking away so he needs to do something now.

- Honor is important, except with a leader like Saul.

- If an action brings promotion, it is always the will of God.

- God is always more concerned about our vision than our character.

Elevating Truths

1. **Our response to our leader's failures reveals how ready we are to really lead** – David's refusal to "stretch out his hand against the Lord's anointed" tells much about the depth of God's work in his life.

2. **God takes His time in developing great leaders** – It may have seemed like a waste of 30 years to have Jesus come to earth as a baby, but God is more interested in developing the minister than the ministry. He takes His time to insure that the load-bearing capacity of the leader is sufficient for the assignment ahead and gives ample opportunity for growth.

3. **Leaders live at a higher level than the people around them** – This is what makes them leaders. David's men encouraged him to kill Saul, but David knew that there was something more important than having a position or even a promise fulfilled (which was to have integrity and to follow the higher perspectives the Lord had shown him).

Giving God Something to Work With

- **Encourage a leader** in your life that you have not encouraged recently.
- **Speak positive things about authority figures** that others are criticizing.
- **Pray** for all who are in authority.

Declarations to Create Higher Perspectives

I honor leaders.

I am a strength to leaders in their area of weakness.

I walk in integrity.

you give them something to eat

"When it was evening, His disciples came to Him, saying, 'This is a deserted place, and the hour is already late. Send the multitudes away, that they may go into the villages and buy themselves food.' But Jesus said to them, 'They do not need to go away. You give them something to eat.' And they said to Him, 'We have here only five loaves and two fish.' He said, 'Bring them here to Me.'... So they all ate and were filled, and they took up twelve baskets full of the fragments that remained. Now those who had eaten were about five thousand men, besides women and children."

Matthew 14:15-21

Lower Perspectives

The disciples could have concluded:

- Jesus would never ask them to do something this "impossible."

- Jesus is only setting them up for failure so they could mature more.

- Children never have the answer for big needs.

- If Jesus really knew them, He would not believe in them so much.

- Jesus would never multiply food because that would be using the supernatural for something other than healing, deliverance or salvation.

- The people should be fasting anyway. If they were more spiritual, they would not even have noticed their hunger.

Elevating Truths

1. **Our capacity to miraculously meet needs is bigger than we know** – The disciples said, "Send the multitudes away." They thought they were not equipped for such a big "ministry," but they were. We too are more ready to be the answer for multitudes

than we think.

2. **God has delegated His authority to us to do miracles** – A law officer who constantly asks his superior to come to his location to arrest people is unwise or ignorant; yet, that is in essence what we do when we ask God to do things we have been given authority to do. "(Jesus) gave (the disciples) power over unclean spirits... and... disease" (Matthew 10:1).

3. **Unlikely people around us hold the key to breakthrough** – The boy with the fish and loaves was not in the inner circle of influential people, but he was the solution for a great need. Let us look beyond outward appearances in people to find the answer for what is being believed for.

Giving God Something to Work With

- **When praying for healing, speak to the sickness** instead of asking God to heal.

- **Consider unlikely people** to be used in a miracle or task.

- **Involve children** in your ministry and organization.

Declarations to Create Higher Perspectives

I have a great capacity to miraculously meet needs.

I empower children and "unknowns" into greatness.

I am an instrument of God's delegated authority.

36 my God shall supply all your need according to His riches

"For even in Thessalonica you sent aid once and again for my necessities. Not that I seek the gift, but I seek the fruit that abounds to your account. Indeed I have all and abound. I am full, having received from Epaphroditus the things sent from you, a sweet-smelling aroma, an acceptable sacrifice, well pleasing to God. **And my God shall supply all your need according to His riches in glory by Christ Jesus***" (Philippians 4:16-19). We serve the God of more than enough. We truly cannot out give God.

Lower Perspectives

Paul could have concluded:

- God is the God of just enough.

- God will supply all their needs according to their level of good works.

- God will supply all their needs except during a recession.

- God will meet all their financial needs, but has limited resources to meet their emotional, relational, physical or other needs.

Elevating Truths

1. **God supplies to us according to the standard of His own wealth** – God will provide riches according to the measure of His own personal wealth and abundance. God's abundance is limitless because it is based on the capital of heaven's economy. "I have come that they may have life, and that they may have it more abundantly" (John 10:10).

2. **God wants to abundantly supply for every need in your life** – He is concerned about ALL of our needs. He wants to lavish on us abundance in every area of need and desire in our lives.

3. **When we give, the kingdom multiplication principle is activated** – "Now may He who supplies seed to the sower... supply and multiply the seed you have sown... " (2 Corinthians 9:10). God takes what we give and supernaturally increases it.

Giving God Something to Work With

- **Speak directly to any mountains of lack** and declare them a place of abundance.

- **Give to someone** in an area where you have need.

- **Express thankfulness to God** in the areas of your life where He has provided. Thankfulness brings increase.

Declarations to Create Higher Perspectives

I live in supernatural abundance in every area of my life.

God's riches are currently being released and multiplied financially, spiritually, relationally, and in all areas of my life.

I am a generous and cheerful giver.

*"And when Saul had come to Jerusalem, he tried to join the disciples; but they were all afraid of him, and did not believe that he was a disciple. **But Barnabas took him and brought him to the apostles.** And he declared to them how he had seen the Lord on the road, and that He had spoken to him, and how he had preached boldly at Damascus in the name of Jesus. So he was with them at Jerusalem, coming in and going out."*

Acts 9:26-28

Lower Perspectives

Barnabas could have concluded:

- If the other Christians didn't trust Saul, he must not be trustworthy.

- If Jesus expects them to receive their arch-enemy, He's going to have to give them their own "Damascus Road Experience" to prove it.

- Saul's story of such a radical conversion could not possibly be true; therefore he must be a counterfeit.

- Even if it was true, associating with Saul would ruin his reputation.

- Saul may have really gotten saved, but a man with such a bad past probably would not make it long enough to be worth the investment.

Elevating Truths

1. **I primarily seek favor with God before seeking favor with man** – Because Barnabas feared God and not man, the world was changed forever. "The fear of man brings a snare, but whoever trusts in the LORD shall be safe" (Proverbs 29:25). "The fear of the LORD is a fountain of life, to turn one away from the snares of death" (Proverbs 14:27).

2. **Keeping Heaven's perspective will take us higher in God** – "For the LORD does not see as man sees; for man looks at the outward appearance, but the LORD looks at the heart" (1 Samuel 16:7). God sees greatness in everyone. Knowing this can thrust people from potential to fulfillment.

3. **Inspiring people to surpass us multiplies our fruit** – The more we empower others, the greater the mission we will accomplish. "He who believes in Me, the works that I do he will do also; and greater works than these he will do, because I go to My Father" (John 14:12).

Giving God Something to Work With

- **Draw out the gold in people** and not the dirt.
- **Look for hidden revivalists** and give them opportunities.
- **Work yourself out of a job** by investing in others.

Declarations to Create Higher Perspectives

I fear God and nothing else.

My prophetic declarations advance people into their destinies.

My decisions open doors for radical revival movements.

38

and Abraham
believed in the Lord

Abraham, the father of our faith, lived a life of obedience and risk. His life was marked by God's promises, his belief and God's faithfulness. God visited him in a dream at the age of 75. *"Then He brought him outside and said, 'Look now toward heaven, and count the stars if you are able to number them.' And He said to him, 'So shall your descendants be.'* **And he believed in the LORD,** *and He accounted it to him for righteousness"*

Genesis 15:5-6

Lower Perspectives

Abraham could have concluded:

- His belief in God's promise had nothing to do with its fulfillment.

- He was childless despite his many years of prayers for a descendant. Why would it happen now?

- He and Sarah were WAY past childbearing years, and it would make much more sense for them to adopt.

- God was using exaggeration for effect when He said their descendants would be as numerous as the stars.

- Believing God's promises about him would not affect his spiritual DNA; it would only affect what he was believing for.

Elevating Truths

1. **Faith is the seedbed of promise** – "Now faith is the substance of things hoped for, the evidence of things not seen" (Hebrews 11:1). Faith is a strong belief, and our faith is the good soil that God uses to germinate His seeds of promise in our lives. When we take responsibility for our beliefs, God takes responsibility for the fulfillment of the promise.

2. **God's promises gain compound interest over time** – David was a young boy when he was promised that he would be king.

At the age of 30, the fulfillment of that promise came and was much more far-reaching than he or anyone around him had ever imagined. In fact David was in the direct lineage of Jesus. (See 2 Samuel 5:1-5.)

3. **Personal transformation comes through belief transformation** – Romans 12:2 says that transformation comes through the renewing of the mind. Beliefs not only forerun experience, they affect our DNA. Abraham, in believing, was not only partnering to bring forth his promise, but he actually changed his identity and his faith (beliefs) was reckoned unto him as righteousness.

Giving God Something to Work With

- **Blow the dust off an old promise** and dream again.
- **Believe and declare** that YOUR promise is gaining compound interest for you in the waiting period.

Declarations to Create Higher Perspectives

God brings His promises to pass.

I am a person of great faith.

My renewed beliefs transform me.

*"Now these were the numbers of the divisions that were equipped for war, and came to David at Hebron... of the sons of Judah bearing shield and spear, six thousand eight hundred armed for war... **of the sons of Issachar who had understanding of the times,** to know what Israel ought to do, their chiefs were two hundred."*

1 Chronicles 12:23-32

Lower Perspectives

David could have concluded:

- God would not bring any new people into his midst who would contribute significantly in the future because God is not that good.

- He should only be guided by principles, not by a "now" word of the Lord.

- He should only trust his own perceptions in determining what needs to be emphasized in a particular period of time.

- He should focus on the same things in every season of his life.

- God would never alter anything He has told him in the past.

- Those with high IQ's are needed for success, but those with strong spiritual perception are unnecessary.

Elevating Truths

1. **We can know the times and seasons for our own lives** – God generously gives special wisdom to each one who asks. (See James 1:5.) This wisdom is often an awareness of what is being emphasized in a particular season of our lives – there will be seasons like building trust, breaking off lies, "mega-doses" of God's word that will grow us in God.

2. **God has uniquely gifted some with great spiritual perception –** We all can hear from the Lord, but some are especially gifted in discerning the "now" word." Having then gifts differing according to the grace that is given to us, let us use them: if prophecy, let us prophesy in proportion to our faith" (Romans 12:6).

3. **We need the prophetically gifted to speak into our lives, ministries, organizations, and nations –** The Old Testament had prophets who spoke into the "times and seasons" of nations and individuals (e.g. Elijah, Elisha, Isaiah, Daniel, etc.). God is still raising up great prophetic voices with favor to speak profound insight to kings and presidents.

Giving God Something to Work With

- **Activate James 1:5-8** by believing God will speak to you with a "now" word.
- **Build relationships** with prophetically gifted people.
- **Identify the season you are in** and the things to focus on.

Declarations to Create Higher Perspectives

I understand times and seasons.

God has put prophetically gifted people in my life and ministry.

I speak prophetically into the "seasons" of others.

"Then David said to his men, 'Every man gird on his sword'... One of the young men told Abigail, Nabal's wife, saying, 'Look, David sent messengers from the wilderness to greet our master; and he reviled them'... Then Abigail made haste... When Abigail saw David, she... said... 'The LORD has held you back from coming to bloodshed and from avenging yourself with your own hand... **For the LORD will certainly make for my lord an enduring house,** *because my lord fights the battles of the LORD... (God) has appointed you ruler over Israel'... Then David said to Abigail... 'blessed is your advice and blessed are you, because you have kept me this day from coming to bloodshed.'"*

1 Samuel 25:13-33

Lower Perspectives

Abigail could have concluded:

- Her husband was a fool, and she was destined to live in turmoil as a result of his poor decisions.

- David had the right to take Nabal's life, and that would solve all her struggles with him.

- David could make his own choices and reap the consequences of them.

- She was a victim to the choices of those around her.

- There was nothing she could do to change the situation.

Elevating Truths

1. **It is worth taking a risk for the sake of another's prophetic destiny** – Abigail recognized God's calling on David and risked her life to see it come to pass. "For the LORD will certainly make for my lord an enduring house, because my lord fights the battles of the LORD" (1 Samuel 25:28).

2. **We are never alone in the battle** – Abigail reminded David that he didn't need to operate in self-protection. Though we may feel alone, God is always fighting on our behalf. "Yet a man has risen to pursue you and seek your life, but the life of my lord shall be bound in the bundle of the living with the LORD your God" (1 Samuel 25:29).

3. **Honor opens the door for influence** – When we walk in honor, those around us are willing to listen, understanding we have their best interest in mind. "So David received from her hand what she had brought him, and said to her, 'I have heeded your voice'" (1 Samuel 25:35).

Giving God Something to Work With

- **Make yourself aware of the prophetic destinies** of those around you.

- **Be willing to put your fears aside** in order to pull out the greatness in others.

- **Recognize you have the power** to bring solutions to even the most difficult problems.

Declarations to Create Higher Perspectives

I help those around me move toward their destiny.

I bring hope and encouragement to all in my life.

I see people's prophetic destiny and call them into it.

41 then Isaac sowed in famine, and reaped a hundredfold

"There was a famine in the land... Then the LORD appeared to him and said: 'Do not go down to Egypt; live in the land of which I shall tell you. Dwell in this land, and I will be with you and bless you... I will give to your descendants all these lands; and in your seed all the nations of the earth shall be blessed'... **Then Isaac sowed in that land, and reaped in the same year a hundredfold;** *and the LORD blessed him. The man began to prosper, and continued prospering until he became very prosperous."*

Genesis 26:1-13

Lower Perspectives

Isaac could have concluded:

- God would never ask him to do anything that seemed illogical.

- In times of economic challenge, there are no supernatural solutions.

- God's remedies always take a long time so he should just go to Egypt.

- It is safer to follow the steps of those who have gone before him than to try new things that are "out of the box."

- If he really believed, he would not have to sow anything.

Elevating Truths

1. **It's smarter to trust that God is smarter** – It would have seemed logical for Isaac to escape the famine like his wise father had done before. However, Isaiah 55:9 tells us that God's ways and thoughts are higher than ours. God had a higher way for Isaac, and He has a higher perspective on what is best for us. As we believe this, His specific wisdom is released to us.

2. **Our faith is what causes us to be an overcomer** – Hebrews 11 tells of ordinary men and women of faith who overcame

challenging circumstances. "For whatever is born of God overcomes the world. And this is the victory that has overcome the world—our faith" (I John 5:4).

3. **It's more blessed to pursue God than to pursue better opportunities** – Jesus promised great provision to His followers. "But seek first the kingdom of God and His righteousness, and all these things shall be added to you" (Matthew 6:33). Putting God first opens up the best of opportunities.

Giving God Something to Work With

- **Meditate and declare scriptures** that promise providence and blessing.

- **Learn from people who have overcome great odds** and have stepped into the realm of "impossibility."

- **Believe God** for all your needs.

Declarations to Create Higher Perspectives

I courageously take risks bigger than my past experiences.

Incredible provision follows my faith-filled decisions.

I overflow with abundance, and I am a famine buster.

42 but at midnight Paul and Silas were praying and singing

"But at midnight Paul and Silas were praying and singing hymns to God... Suddenly there was a great earthquake... and immediately all the doors were opened and everyone's chains were loosed. And the keeper of the prison, awaking from sleep and seeing the prison doors open, supposing the prisoners had fled, drew his sword and was about to kill himself. But Paul called with a loud voice, saying, 'Do yourself no harm, for we are all here.' Then he... said, 'Sirs, what must I do to be saved?'"

Acts 16:25-30

Lower Perspectives

Paul and Silas could have concluded:

- They had a right to throw themselves a royal pity party.

- They no longer had any influence because they were in prison.

- They should only sing and praise in church or else they could be considered fanatical.

- They should be very discouraged because we should never experience a trial if we are in the will of God.

- They would probably just die there in jail, so they should give up.

Elevating Truths

1. **Rejoicing and gratefulness release breakthrough** – "Rejoice in the Lord always" (Philippians 4:4). "Now the Lord is the Spirit; and where the Spirit of the Lord is, there is liberty" (2 Corinthians 3:17). Giving thanks and praising God takes us to a place far above our trials.

2. **God's presence is stronger than any attack or discouragement** – "But you are holy, enthroned in the praises of Israel" (Psalm 22:3). "But the night shines as the day; the darkness and the light are

both alike to You" (Psalm 139:12). When we wrap ourselves in His presence, we do not have to fear unexpected detours that may occur along the journey.

3. **There is something more valuable than having comfortable circumstances** – Paul and Silas had become assured of their eternal life in Jesus, so the fear of dying had been broken off of them. "Whoever believes in Him should not perish but have everlasting life" (John 3:16). The promise of peace, joy, and everlasting life became a great force of breakthrough.

Giving God Something to Work With

- **When facing an unexpected trial,** verbally thank God.
- **When you are tempted to become discouraged,** turn your affections towards Him.
- **Declare His goodness** and character over your trials.

Declarations to Create Higher Perspectives

I am a thankful worshipper no matter what the circumstances.

I believe that He who dwells in me is greater than He who dwells in this world.

God inhabits my praise.

43 there is no other name by which you must be saved

*"Then Peter, filled with the Holy Spirit, said to them... 'Let it be known to you all, and to all the people of Israel, that by the name of Jesus Christ of Nazareth... this man stands here before you whole... Nor is there salvation in any other, for **there is no other name under heaven given among men by which we must be saved.'** Now when they saw the boldness of Peter and John, and perceived that they were uneducated and untrained men, they marveled. And they realized that they had been with Jesus"*

Acts 4:8-13

Lower Perspectives

Peter could have concluded:

- It would be politically incorrect to make such a statement.

- Jesus' death and resurrection was not that big of a deal; thus, there was no need to get too worked up about it.

- All religions are the same so he should say that the name of Jesus was one of many names that could get them saved.

- He should water down his message so that more would accept it.

- Being saved is simply trying to be more religious, not a transformation of his life by the power of God.

Elevating Truths

1. **The Tomb really is empty** – The disciples absolutely believed Jesus rose from the dead. There is no other explanation for their willingness to die for saying He was alive. "And if Christ is not risen, then our preaching is empty and your faith is also empty" (I Corinthians 15:14).

2. **Jesus is God** – "For in Him dwells all the fullness of the Godhead bodily" (Colossians 2:9). Jesus said, "He who has seen Me has

seen the Father" (John 14:9). God came to earth as a man. Life begins when we believe this and see all of history as "His story."

3. **We all must receive salvation through the name of Jesus** – "Jesus answered and said to him, 'Most assuredly, I say to you, unless one is born again, he cannot see the kingdom of God'" (John 3:3). "For God so loved the world that He gave His only begotten Son, that whoever believes in Him should not perish but have everlasting life" (John 3:16).

Giving God Something to Work With

- **Read** and re-read John 3:1-16.
- **Receive training** in evangelism.
- **Seek out testimonies of people** who have been born again in Christ.

Declarations to Create Higher Perspectives

Jesus is the only name through which we can be saved.

I lead people to Christ on a regular basis.

I strongly value my own conversion testimony and those of others.

44

please test your servants for ten days

""Then the king instructed... the master of his eunuchs, to bring some of the children of Israel... who had the ability to serve in the king's palace... And the king appointed for them a daily provision of the king's delicacies... and three years of training for them, so that at the end of that time they might serve before the king... But Daniel purposed in his heart that he would not defile himself with the portion of the king's delicacies... So Daniel said... **'Please test your servants for ten days, and let them give us vegetables to eat and water to drink.** *Then let our appearance be examined before you... ' And at the end of ten days their features appeared better and fatter in flesh than all the young men who ate the portion of the king's delicacies."*

Daniel 1:3-15

Lower Perspectives

Daniel could have concluded:

- Honoring God would only bless him in heaven, and never on earth.

- Pleasing his leaders, even when unethical, is always good to do.

- Blending in, and the path of least resistance, is God's will for us.

- If a course of action is not logical, then it could not be from God.

- He should always distance himself from any leader that is ungodly.

- God does not give astoundingly superior wisdom to His people.

Elevating Truths

1. **Our prosperity on earth matters to God** – In Genesis 1:28, after God creates man, He commissions them to subdue the earth and have dominion over it. He has always wanted His sons and daughters to be royalty in the world He placed us on. It's a laughable lie that God wants His sons and daughters to be

Higher
PERSPECTIVES

unsuccessful and ruled by darkness.

2. **Heavenly laws trump natural laws** – As believers, we are dual-citizens of both heaven and earth. Although it can be easy to be solely focused on this natural world we see, it is key to realize that the invisible is more real than the visible. We are supernatural by nature.

3. **God isn't scared of positioning the godly under the ungodly** – In the Sermon on the Mount in Matthew 5, Jesus uses metaphors of salt and light to speak of Christians. It is our nature to shift our surroundings, not be shifted. We are ambassadors of heaven and agents of change.

Giving God Something to Work With

- **Unashamedly position yourself to be blessed** in every area of your life.
- **Find an opportunity to joyfully serve** a non-believer.
- **Do a creative 10-day fast.**

Declarations to Create Higher Perspectives

I am an agent of change to the world around me.

God loves to bless me in all areas of my life.

I am positioned for great things everywhere I go.

45 I planted, Apollos watered, but God gave the increase

*"Who then is Paul, and who is Apollos, but ministers through whom you believed, as the Lord gave to each one? **I planted, Apollos watered, but God gave the increase.** So then neither he who plants is anything, nor he who waters, but God who gives the increase."*

1 Corinthians 3:5-7

Lower Perspectives

Paul could have concluded:

- Once he discovered his own leadership style and ministry emphasis, then he should look down on those who minister differently.

- There are only two worthwhile roles in the kingdom: pioneers and harvesters. Everything in between is an unimportant function.

- God most credits whoever is present the moment the fruit comes forth.

- Apollos was only successful because he built on what he (Paul) already started.

Elevating Truths

1. **Every Christian has a crucial role in kingdom expansion** – God reveals His creative expression through each uniquely crafted person, causing the entire Body to grow up into Christ, the Head. "According to the effective working by which every part does its share, causes growth of the body for the edifying of itself in love" (Ephesians 4:16).

2. **Partnering with others expands God's opportunities** – God reserves the commanded blessing for those who put aside their differences and gather together around Jesus Christ. "Behold,

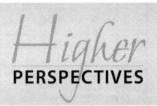

how good and how pleasant it is for brethren to dwell together in unity... For there the LORD commanded the blessing–Life forevermore" (Psalm 133).

3. **Bringing our natural abilities to God creates supernatural results** – Our offerings to God are weak at best; but in love, He unites us with omnipotence. "He said to me, 'My grace is sufficient for you, for My strength is made perfect in weakness.' Therefore most gladly I will rather boast in my infirmities, that the power of Christ may rest upon me... For when I am weak, then I am strong" (2 Corinthians 12:9-10).

Giving God Something to Work With

- **Discover God's beauty** in the people around you and find ways to affirm it.

- **Find someone you would typically avoid** and encourage them in their walk with the Lord.

- **Spend time praising God** for the soon coming breakthrough in a ministry you have been serving.

Declarations to Create Higher Perspectives

I am significant in the Kingdom of God.

I demolish walls and build bridges within the Body of Christ.

I am supernatural and do exploits beyond my human abilities.

46 let us go up at once, for we are well able to overcome it

*"And the LORD spoke to Moses, 'Send men to spy out the land of Canaan'... Then they told him 'We went to the land... It truly flows with milk and honey... the cities are fortified... we saw the descendants of Anak there (the descendants came from the giants).' Then Caleb quieted the people before Moses, and said, '**Let us go up at once and take possession, for we are well able to overcome it.**"*

Numbers 13:1-30

Lower Perspectives

Caleb could have concluded:

- The opinion of the majority will always reflect God's will.
- God would never have him do anything that seems impossible.
- Avoidance of the giants is worth losing the promise land.
- They were unworthy sinners with no power to overcome giants.
- He should not make such a bold declaration if he is in the minority.

Elevating Truths

1. **The giants were already conquered in the land** – "But thanks be to God, who gives us the victory through our Lord Jesus Christ" (1 Corinthians 15:57). Our victory was already sealed through Jesus. We are not still trying to conquer our giants. We ARE taking possession of our own Promised Land that has already been credited to our accounts through the price Christ paid.

2. **Beliefs determine our future** – "Surely none of the men... shall see the land...except Caleb and Joshua for they have wholly followed the Lord" (Numbers 32:11-12). Caleb's belief that he already had the victory resulted in him eventually gaining entrance into the Promised Land, while the people's unbelief

Higher
PERSPECTIVES

kept them from moving forward.

3. **True sons and daughters live in their promise land** – "But you received the Spirit of adoption by whom we cry out, 'Abba, Father'" (Romans 8:15). People who know their true identity in Christ live at high hope levels until the awaited promise catches up with their mindsets. Our good Father only wants what is best for His children.

Giving God Something to Work With

- **Speak out what you want to materialize** and not necessarily what you currently see.

- **Identify something that appears to be a giant in your life** and gain God's perspective of victory.

- **Meditate on your position as a son or daughter** in Christ.

Declarations to Create Higher Perspectives

I am victorious in ALL areas of my life.

I am a child of God.

I live in the Father's blessing continually.

47 unless you are converted and become as little children

*"At that time the disciples came to Jesus, saying, 'Who then is greatest in the kingdom of heaven?' Then Jesus called a little child to Him, set him in the midst of them, and said, 'Assuredly, I say to you, **unless you are converted and become as little children,** you will by no means enter the kingdom of heaven. Therefore whoever humbles himself as this little child is the greatest in the kingdom of heaven'"*

Matthew 18:1-4

Lower Perspectives

Jesus could have concluded:

- Children are cute, but they don't carry much weight in the kingdom.

- One's size represents the amount of spiritual power that can be contained.

- Children should be neither seen nor heard, especially while important spiritual people are speaking.

- Blessed are the serious adults for they will recognize the kingdom.

- As people grow older, they should leave their childish idealism behind.

- There is nothing spiritually profound we can learn from children.

Elevating Truths

1. **Sincerity of heart affects our ability to connect to God more than our age** – "Blessed [are] the pure in heart for they shall see God" (Matthew 5:8). "For the LORD does not see as man sees; for man looks at the outward appearance, but the LORD looks at the heart" (1 Samuel 16:7). Relationship with God is about the position of our hearts rather than our outward appearances.

2. **Simplicity is a way of the kingdom** – "But one thing is needed, and Mary has chosen that good part, which will not be taken away from her" (Luke 10:42). Children have an innate ability to live free from the world's complexities and to single-mindedly focus on the task before them.

3. **Like children, we are created to live in eager anticipation** – "Now faith is the substance of things hoped for, the evidence of things not seen" (Hebrews 11:1). Children expect great things! They eagerly await Christmas morning, trusting that their parents will continually exceed their expectations for good gifts. They are our example for living.

Giving God Something to Work With

- **Be quick to forgive.**
- **Build the "muscle" of enthusiasm** by intentionally acting more enthusiastic than you feel.
- **Find joy in the simple** and small things.

Declarations to Create Higher Perspectives

I am becoming increasingly childlike.

I am free to love God and others.

Like children, I laugh often.

48 a hundredfold now in this time

*"Assuredly, I say to you, there is no one who has left house or brothers or sisters or father or mother or wife or children or lands, for My sake and the gospel's, who shall not receive **a hundredfold now in this time** –houses and brothers and sisters and mothers and children and lands, with persecutions – and in the age to come, eternal life."*

Mark 10:29-30

Lower Perspectives
We could conclude:

- Living for Jesus will make us miserable in this life.

- Investing in stocks creates wealth more reliably than investing in God.

- Because abundance is God's will for me, my choices and beliefs cannot hinder His plan.

- If something feels sacrificial, it cannot be God's will for us.

- God is happiest with people who don't have much.

Elevating Truths

1. **When we partner with Jesus, He foots the bill** – God will never call us into places without promising to abundantly provide the means to get us there. "Seek first the kingdom of God and His righteousness, and all these things shall be added to you" (Matthew 6:33).

2. **Investing in eternity creates present realities** – When we surrender our all to heaven, we gain a connection we can draw from now. "Lay up for yourselves treasures in heaven, where neither moth nor rust destroys and where thieves do not break in and steal. For where your treasure is, there your heart will be also" (Matthew 6:20-21).

3. **Heaven's exchange rate far outweighs our sacrifices** – Offerings that seem painful always trade up with God, yielding great returns. "Give, and it will be given to you: good measure, pressed down, shaken together, and running over will be put into your bosom. For with the same measure that you use, it will be measured back to you" (Luke 6:38).

Giving God Something to Work With

- **Find a way to bless someone** with something you value.
- **Identify the measure of faith you have** in an area of importance and take one step beyond.
- **Invite your loved ones to partner** with the mission you've been called to.

Declarations to Create Higher Perspectives

There is not a selfish bone in my body.

My Daddy supplies all my needs according to His riches in glory.

There is nothing I can't do for the Kingdom of God!

for to me, to live is Christ, and to die is gain

*"**For to me, to live is Christ, and to die is gain.** But if I live on in the flesh, this will mean fruit from my labor... For I am hard-pressed between the two, having a desire to depart and be with Christ, which is far better. Nevertheless to remain in the flesh is more needful for you. And being confident of this, I know that I shall remain and continue with you all for your progress and joy of faith"*

Philippians 1:21-25

Lower Perspectives

Paul could have concluded:

- Death is something to be feared for the Christian.

- Self-gratification should be the greatest consideration in his decision.

- His life and ministry had no lasting impact on others.

- Even if there is a heaven, it would be an inferior experience than earth.

- The Body of Christ can function well without all its parts.

- A greater call or destiny in life is an unrealistic expectation.

Elevating Truths

1. **Fullness of life in Christ is now** – "And the Word became flesh... and of His fullness we have all received" (John 1:14-16). To live IS Christ. We are the righteousness of Christ and were born to do greater works than He did here and now. We are not waiting for heaven to experience full life.

2. **We are all vital parts of the body** – "But now God has set the members... in the body just as He pleases... And the eye cannot say to the hand, 'I have no need of you'" (I Corinthians 12:18-21). When parts aren't present or functioning in the body, atrophy

occurs. The church reaches its highest potential when all the parts are working together.

3. **Death has lost its sting** – "For the trumpet will sound... and we will be changed... Death is swallowed up in victory" (I Corinthians 15:52-54). When we leave this earth, we are just continuing our intimate relationship with Christ into eternity. At death, we enter a perfect union with Christ in the physical realm that we've been experiencing spiritually. To die truly is gain.

Giving God Something to Work With

- **Meditate on the truth that** "to die is gain" in accordance to your current union with Christ, gaining perfection in heaven.

- **Identify some lies that you believe** about who you are and replace them with truth.

- **Identify your role in the Body of Christ** and function in it.

Declarations to Create Higher Perspectives

I am a vital part of the Body of Christ with unique gifts and calling.

As a believer, I live with the hope that to die really is gain.

I have complete union with Christ through His sacrifice.

50

whatever He says to you, do it

*"And when they ran out of wine, the mother of Jesus said to Him, 'They have no wine.' Jesus said to her, 'Woman, what does your concern have to do with Me? **My hour has not yet come.'** His mother said to the servants, **'Whatever He says to you, do it.'**... Jesus said to them, 'Fill the water pots with water.'... When the master of the feast had tasted the water that was made wine,... (he) called the bridegroom. And he said to him, 'Every man at the beginning sets out the good wine, and when the guests have well drunk, then the inferior. You have kept the good wine until now!'"*

John 2:3-10

Lower Perspectives

Mary could have concluded:

- There would be no miracle if Jesus said it was not time for one.

- She would be in rebellion to think more of the possibility of a miracle.

- It was not the proper time for something so supernatural to happen.

- God has predestined our lives with specific limits on them.

- She could never change God's mind.

Elevating Truths

1. **We can bring future promises into the present** – Abraham had a new covenant experience in the Old Covenant. (See Genesis 15:6). David brought the future to his life by moving past sacrificing animals to worship as the means to connect with God. The Syrophoenician woman accelerated salvation coming to Gentiles through her response to Jesus' initial denial of her need (see Mark 7:25-30). Mary's response at the wedding adds to this list. We too can do the same.

2. **We can influence God** – Moses did this in Exodus 32 when the Lord said He was going to destroy His people. The people of Ninevah reversed God's declared judgment over them by repenting after hearing Jonah's message. What is pronounced is not always the final word on a matter, but it is often an invitation to the discerning to ignite a miracle.

3. **We can cause "unplanned" miracles to happen** – Mary believed that if God was not "moving," she would do something so that He would. Let's believe there is always a way to bring a miracle into a situation.

Giving God Something to Work With

- **Develop an insatiable hunger** to see things on earth as they are in heaven.
- **Believe all things are possible** to those who believe.
- **Pull on the promises of God.**

Declarations to Create Higher Perspectives

I accelerate the timing of heavenly blessings being released.

I cause unexpected miracles to happen.

I persevere in seeing miracles happen.

additional resources
by Steve & Wendy Backlund

Victorious Mindsets

What we believe is ultimately more important than what we do. The course of our lives is set by our deepest core beliefs. Our mindsets are either a stronghold for God's purposes or a playhouse for the enemy. In this book, fifty biblical attitudes are revealed that are foundational for those who desire to walk in freedom and power.

Cracks in the Foundation

Going to a higher level in establishing key beliefs will affect ones intimacy with God and fruitfulness for the days ahead. This book challenges many basic assumptions of familiar Bible verses and common Christian phrases that block numerous benefits of our salvation. The truths shared in this book will help fill and repair "cracks" in our thinking which rob us of our God-given potential.

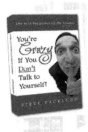

You're Crazy If You Don't Talk to Yourself

Jesus did not just think His way out of the wilderness and neither can we. He spoke truth to invisible beings and mindsets that sought to restrict and defeat Him. This book reveals that life and death are truly in the power of the tongue, and emphasize the necessity of speaking truth to our souls. Our words really do set the course of our lives and the lives of others. (Proverbs 18:21; James 3:2-5)

Let's Just Laugh at That

Our hope level is an indicator of whether we are believing truth or lies. Truth creates hope and freedom, but believing lies brings hopelessness and restriction. We can have great theology but still be powerless because of deception about the key issues of life.

additional resources
by Steve & Wendy Backlund

Many of these self-defeating mindsets exist in our subconscious and have never been identified. This book exposes numerous falsehoods and reveals truth that makes us free. Get ready for a joy-infused adventure into hope-filled living.

Divine Strategies for Increase

The laws of the spirit are more real than the natural laws. God's laws are primarily principles to release blessing, not rules to be obeyed to gain right standing with God. The Psalmist talks of one whose greatest delight is in the law of the Lord. This delight allows one to discover new aspects of the nature of God (hidden in each law) to behold and worship. The end result of this delighting is a transformed life that prospers in every endeavor. His experience can be our experience, and this book unlocks the blessings hidden in the spiritual realm.

Possessing Joy

In His presence is fullness of joy (Psalm 16:11). Joy is to increase as we go deeper in our relationship with God. Religious tradition has devalued the role that gladness and laughter have for personal victory and kingdom advancement. His presence may not always produce joy; but if we never or rarely have fullness of joy, we must reevaluate our concept of God. This book takes one on a journey toward the headwaters of the full joy that Jesus often spoke of. Get ready for joy to increase and strength and longevity to ignite.

additional resources
by Steve & Wendy Backlund

Igniting Faith in 40 Days

There must be special seasons in our lives when we break out of routine and do something that will ignite our faith about God and our identity in Christ. This book will lead you through the life-changing experience of a 40-day negativity fast. This fast teaches the power of declaring truth and other transforming daily customs that will strengthen your foundation of faith and radically increase your personal hope.

Living From The Unseen

This book will help you identify beliefs that block the reception of God's blessings and hinder our ability to live out our destiny. This book reveals that 1) Believing differently, not trying harder, is the key to change; 2) You cannot do what you don't believe you are.; 3) You can only receive what you think you are worth; 4) Rather than learning how to die - it is time to learn how to live..

Audio message series are available through the Igniting Hope store at: www.IgnitedHope.com.